Shields of Brass

C. ROY ANGELL

shields of brass

BROADMAN PRESS
Nashville, Tennessee

© 1965 • BROADMAN PRESS
All rights reserved

Larger Type Edition

4251-72
ISBN: 0-8054-5172-2

DEWEY DECIMAL CLASSIFICATION NUMBER: 252
Library of Congress catalog card number: 65–19548
Printed in the United States of America

Contents

1
Shields of Brass

Buried in the fourteenth chapter of 1 Kings is a tragic symbol of Christianity today. The historian relates how the Egyptians captured Jerusalem and "took away the treasures of the house of the Lord, and the treasures of the king's house; he even took away all: and he took away all the shields of gold which Solomon had made. And king Rehoboam made in their stead brasen [brass] shields, and committed them unto the hands of the chief of the guard, which kept the door of the king's house" (vv. 26–27). The very same sentence is repeated in the twelfth chapter of 2 Chronicles.

Those shields of gold were never meant to be used in war. They had a special mission. They were brought out of the vault only when the king went to the Temple to worship. It seems the guard formed a double line, holding the shields to form a gold enclosed pathway for the king. There were three hundred of them and they had been made by Solomon when he built the Temple. They were a part of God's design. It was as if the Temple held out its arms to welcome the worshiper. It created a spiritual atmosphere and made a hush fall over those who silently followed their monarch into God's house.

7

No shields of brass could ever take the place of those golden shields. This story provokes some timely questions for all of us.

I

Do some Christians substitute the brass of church attendance for the gold of worship?—Carlyle Marney in *These Things Remain* has a stinging rebuke to such people. In a chapter titled "Pronounce the Benediction," he says that to these people "going to church" is a tiresome chore. Impatiently they wait for the minister to "get it over with" and pronounce the benediction. They feel they have fulfilled their religious duty when they attend the Sunday morning service. They don't come to *worship*. They don't come to spend awhile in quiet fellowship with God. Church attendance to them is an "end." It is something they must "perform" to show their dry orthodoxy or to establish their respectability in the community. Elton Trueblood, writing about this same group, has termed them "The Passenger List." He insists that every church member should be a part of the "working crew"; and, if he is not, he is not really a member.

Is this precious hour of worship not very worshipful because the minister who plans the service substitutes brass for the golden message of Jesus? Do ministers sometimes present sermons to make people *feel* good instead of making them *do* good? I know that God is glad this does not happen often, and I know we are all glad that the number of those referred to above is not legion. To most of us, the Sunday service is a golden hour of worship and inspiration. We come in deep reverence to give "the Most High a hearing." We are hungry to draw nearer to God and to let him wash the dross and alloy out of our lives. It hurts something inside of us when some soul-lifting hymn is followed by a battery of announcements about Ping-pong tournaments, oyster suppers, and beach parties. Joseph R. Sizoo asks, "How near can a man who is tired of the strain and stress of business, or a mother who is surfeited with household duties, come to the gates of heaven in such a setting?"

In that most important sixty minutes of worship there should be reverence. Participants should always go out inspired, wanting to do something for the Master.

It was just such a service as this that caused six young ladies to linger awhile and ask each other, "What can we do?" They decided to meet that afternoon for a little prayer meeting. There a beautiful idea was born—one that has blessed thousands of people and led other thousands to Christ.

The next day they went to their pastor and asked if they could have printed some calling cards with a picture of the church on them and an invitation to come and worship with them. Eventually they went out two and two, ringing all the doorbells in the community, giving out the cards and adding their own personal invitation.

At a rooming house near the church, a man read the card and listened to their little speech, shook his head and answered, "You don't want me, I'm a vaudeville actor. No Baptist church would welcome me." After being assured he would be welcome, he finally promised to attend one time, just to prove that they were mistaken. He did attend, again and again and again. He finally gave his heart to Jesus and joined old Walnut Street Baptist Church in Louisville, Kentucky. Later he became pastor of a church in Boston, and it was through his ministry that Russell Conwell felt the call to preach. Conwell has led thousands to Christ and inspired other thousands to a closer walk with God.

When we go up to worship and there is no "brass" in the service wonderful things can happen.

II

Can anything take the place of a church's responsibility to the lost?—God has given us a message more precious than fine gold. It must make him sad when Sunday after Sunday we gather and sing hymns, listen to the announcements of the week's activities, "endure" a sermon, and go home feeling we have done our religious duty for the week. In the book of Revelation, God said to one church, "I have somewhat against thee, because thou hast left thy first love" (2:4). Nothing can take the place of this. We would never want to "become as sounding brass, or a tinkling cymbal" (1 Cor. 13:1). Our God-given assignment is to find and lead to Christ those who are lost. This is our first task. A church has no excuse for existing if people are not being saved. Let me illustrate this with two incidents.

I heard a secretary of evangelism tell of being in a large church one Sunday when the pastor said, "You all know this is the day we have set to finish our drive for funds for a new education plant. Our goal for today is $75,000 in cash—pledges payable in one month!" The chairman of the building fund committee made a ten-minute plea preceding the pastor's sermon, which was titled, "Will a Man Rob God?" After the sermon, the deacons took the offering. Just before the benediction it was announced that the offering far exceeded their goal. There was a round of applause; everybody started hugging and kissing each other. They were so happy that they did not want to go home.

The next Sunday again the minister preached a good sermon. When the invitation was given a twelve-year-old boy walked down the aisle and was received into the church. "Of course," the pastor said, "you will come and welcome this fine boy and tell him you are glad he has accepted Christ." Here

Dr. Meigs stopped and his kind face was sad as he concluded the story with this sentence, "*Eight* people came to shake his hand."

Have we substituted *some things* for the Great Commission God gave us?

Is your pastor so loaded down with administrative duties that he doesn't have time to go out into the "lanes and streets" and talk to the lost people about their soul's needs? Are we filling the lives of our fine Christian laymen so full of meetings that they have no time for personal soul-winning? Not long ago, one of our most consecrated young deacons came into the prayer room just before the morning service. He had a twinkle of mischief in his face as he asked me: "Doctor, can't you think of something for me to do on Friday night? You see, Monday night I have deacons' meeting, Tuesday night a class banquet, and Wednesday night is Family Night and prayer meeting. Thursday night the Boy Scout Committee meets. I don't have a thing to do on Friday night." I wouldn't call any of these things "brass shields," *but they were taking the place of our Lord's Great Commission.* There was no time left in his week to "go out into the highways and the hedges and bring them in."

A traveler just back from a tour of England had a story to tell:

"Among the group of us there was one little old lady who wasn't ever dressed very neatly. Often her clothes were wrinkled, as though they had been packed too tightly in a small suitcase. But no one was as spry as she, and no one got as much out of the tour as she did. When our group went through Westminster Abbey, she stuck close to the guide so she wouldn't miss a thing he said. She was interested in everything. She read aloud the gold leaf words on the pulpit podium: 'We have an advocate.'

"The guide pointed out the places where the King and Queen sat and mentioned the names of many of the royalty who had worshiped here. He closed his discourse with the words (arrogantly spoken), 'This is the most famous pulpit in the world.' After a moment he asked, 'Are there any questions?'

"The dear little old lady's hand went up, 'I have one. Has anybody been saved here lately?'

"The guide's face was a picture of confusion. Finally he asked, 'What was your question? Repeat it, please.'

"Quick as a flash she repeated, in a loud voice, 'Has anybody been saved here lately?' The guide, still confused, took a few moments with his head turned away before he said, 'I've never been asked that question before and I don't know the answer.'"

The teller of this story added: "I travel a lot, and invariably, as I sit in some church for the first time, this question comes back to me, "Has anybody been saved here lately?"

III

Is there any substitute for God's plan of salvation?— Every Christian ought to be a bit indignant at this question. We know that to inherit eternal life we must *believe, repent of sin*, and *accept Christ as our Saviour*. We know there is no other way. Think for a moment. Isn't God sometimes indignant that we, who know this, are so unconcerned about the lost people around us? Aren't there literally millions in our own beloved America who have never been told, or do not believe this to be true? Aren't there multitudes who think there is some other way?

How many times preachers have been told, "My religion is the Golden Rule." There must be millions who think they can substitute *good works* for God's golden plan of salvation.

Good works are only brass shields when we use them as a substitute for Calvary. They will not protect us when we stand before God's judgment bar.

Billy Graham shocked a number of the twenty thousand of us who were listening to him one night after he returned from a campaign in Africa. He said: "We think we are winning the world to Christ. We are *not* winning the world for Christ. We are losing it. We boast of having fifteen hundred foreign missionaries. Did you know that one other denomination has more than fifteen hundred missionaries in *one* country in Africa? We are not even keeping up with the population increase here in America. In Africa, the Mohammedans are making five converts to every one we make."

I say it stunned us. Why were we letting these things happen? I stopped listening to the sermon, for suddenly I had the answer. It was the message contained in a story that I had received. It read about like this:

"A young man had been appointed by the Foreign Mission Board to go to Africa. The thrill was dampened by just one thing. The girl who had been his sweetheart through the years would not marry him if he accepted the appointment. To all of his pleas and reasoning, her answer was a definite no. One month before the time he was to sail he decided to write her one more letter. He hoped something had happened to change her mind. After he wrote it, he added a postscript which read: 'If this letter has made you miserable, just throw it in the waste basket and don't answer it.'

"Something *had* happened, and with a joyous heart she wrote and told him in a dozen different ways she loved him enough to go to the end of the world with him. When she started to the post office to mail it, however, she found it was raining so hard she hesitated, then told her younger brother she would give him a quarter if he would run and mail it.

Anxiously she watched for a wire or a letter. None came. The months dragged by on leaden feet and she learned that he had gone without her. Years later, when the family was moving to another house, she found an old coat that belonged to her brother. In a pocket was her letter."

The story may or may not be true, but this *is* true. God wrote a love letter to lost people and we haven't delivered it. Once in awhile God sends us a reminder. Sometimes it comes in a strange looking package; and sometimes we hug it to our hearts and go do the things God wants us to do.

A deacon came up to my office one day and said: "Preacher, I saw a thing the other day that in a way was funny, but on the other hand it was wonderful. I was driving home on a road through the Everglades. I came around a bend in the road and there was a mother coon and five little baby coons trotting up the road. One was a runt and he was far behind. I drove around him and stopped my car between him and the others. I jumped out and caught him to take him home to my children. He let out one squall and that old mother coon came back in a hurry. She was snarling and coming for a fight with me, a two-hundred-pound man. I put that runt down and ran back down the road. She nudged the baby coon around my car and then stayed in the road between me and the car until the little family was safe in the woods. Preacher, I felt like taking my hat off to her. She would have given her life for that little runt. I stood there in the road and the thought came to me, 'Jesus did give his life for a runt like me.' As I drove along home, I decided I'd really go to work for him." Today a beautiful church stands as a memorial to his dedication.

2
Christ's Recipe for Happiness

In 1921, Lyman Abbott sat in the pastor's study of a big church. He was to review his latest book, *What Christianity Means to Me*. It was forty-five minutes before time for the service and the church was packed to standing room.

The pastor came in and laid his copy of Dr. Abbott's book down in front of the great author and said to him, "Autograph it for me please, and write in it *the ripest thought that you have had in these sixty years of your ministry*."

The pastor went out. Thirty minutes later he came back. Dr. Lyman Abbott still sat, pen in hand, book open in front of him, eyes unfocused, looking off into space. He hadn't written a word. The pastor tiptoed out. Fifteen minutes later he returned. It was time for the service to begin. The ink was not yet dry on the flyleaf of the book. This is what Dr. Abbott had written: "Christianity is not a philosophy that Jesus came to teach. Christianity is a life that Jesus came to impart."

Gaston Foote, one of our finest authors, has said, "I know no better introduction to the Sermon on the Mount than this key which would unlock so much of the teachings of Jesus and so much of the actions of the Christ. He came to impart a life, not to teach a philosophy, not to set up some new school, but to impart a life."

When we open our Bibles to Jesus' great sermon and find it begins with "Blessed . . . ," repeated nine times—there is no question about the predominant note in the life that he came to impart. It is joy, it is blessedness, it is happiness, it is fulfilment—it is a life filled full of light and of living.

So, in this sermon preached on the mountainside, Jesus gave us the structure for a happy, Christian life. When we look at the things he challenged us to do, the words of the grand old poet Browning come to mind, "Your reach should exceed your grasp—or what's a heaven for?" Browning must have meant that when we stand tall, even on tiptoe, we can touch some things that we can never grasp. Perhaps he had been reading the last few verses of the fifth chapter of Matthew. Look at these three statements of the Master Teacher.

I

Whosoever shall smite thee on thy right cheek, turn to him the other also (Matt. 5:39).—Of course, Jesus did not mean this literally. He was stating a great principle: *Don't hit back; don't try to get even; don't seek revenge.* Some people have tried to make this a proof text for pacifism. Jesus was not talking about war, nor was he even thinking of self-defense and the necessity of protecting our nation, our homes, or even our lives. He was pointing out the danger of building up resentments within our minds and seeking some way to hurt someone else a little more than he has hurt us. It was entirely in character, for as Isaiah said, "He was oppressed, and he was afflicted, yet he opened not his mouth: he is brought as a lamb to the slaughter, and as a sheep before her shearers is dumb, so he openeth not his mouth" (53:7). Jesus is underscoring a principle that would add a lot to our happiness.

CHRIST'S RECIPE FOR HAPPINESS

One night after ten o'clock Messineur, the most famous portrait and landscape painter of his time, called one of the most famous physician-surgeons in Paris and said, "Doctor, will you please come over to my house quickly? I have an emergency. I so need you, Doctor, and I don't want anybody else but you. Won't you please come? I know you don't make night calls, and I know you have to operate tomorrow morning, but Doctor make this one exception. Please do. I'll see that you are well paid for it."

The doctor hurried, and when Messineur met him at the door, the surgeon said, "Well, I'm glad to see you are not the patient. You are pretty precious to Paris for your paintings." Quickly they went through room after room in the great mansion until they came to a little sun porch where, among the cushions, lay a tiny poodle with a broken leg. The great surgeon almost froze with astonishment. Then he swallowed his pride—for the time being; opened his bag, set the bone, put the splints on just as carefully and tenderly as if he were ministering to a king. As the doctor prepared to leave, Messineur said, "Doctor, send me a big bill. I don't care how much it is, I'll pay it."

"I'll not send you any bill at all. Come up to my office next week and we'll talk about the payment," the doctor answered. When Messineur arrived the next week the doctor said, "You're a painter, aren't you?"

He answered, "I paint portraits and landscapes."

The surgeon said, "You *are* a painter, aren't you?"

The artist again answered, "I paint portraits and landscapes."

"But," the doctor persisted, "you are a painter, aren't you?"

"Yes sir, I am a painter. I paint portraits and landscapes."

"Well, come with me," said the doctor. They went through three or four rooms until they came to a little room with nothing in it but a cabinet in the middle of the floor which was covered with newspapers. Near the cabinet there was a can of white paint and a cheap brush. "Paint the cabinet and we'll call the bill for the dog square," said the doctor as he turned and walked out.

A little while later the artist came back to the doctor's office and with no resentment in his voice at all asked, "Doctor, are you going to be using that room for the next three or four days?"

"No, take your time. Paint it any time you want to."

"May I have the key to it?" Messineur asked. He locked it up. A few days later the artist came back and smilingly said, "I've finished painting the cabinet. Come and look at it. I hope it suits you." There on the front of that cabinet was what has been called Messineur's masterpiece.

The doctor stood with his mouth open a minute and then with his eyes a little bit misty, stuck out his hand and said, "You're a better man than I am, Gunga Din. I'll take that home and put it in my living room, but I won't tell the world how ugly I was to you."

Now, suppose Messineur had just painted that cabinet white as the doctor suggested. They would have squared off at each other and been enemies the rest of their lives. Instead they became the closest of friends. They made each other happy. That's what Jesus is talking about when he said, "Turn the other cheek."

II

Pray for them which despitefully use you (Matt. 5:44). —Here is one of the hardest things Jesus ever challenged us to do, but no one will dispute that a lot of happiness is wrapped up in it. There was one sentence that used to creep into the sermons Dr. Truett preached at the cowboys' encampment in west Texas. In the four years that I was with him I heard him say it at least a dozen times, "Pray for others and get a blessing for yourself." There was a time, and that not too many years ago, when a pastor was in danger of being called a modernist if he said prayer was *subjective*. But are we just as sure that praying doesn't change us as well as changing things? Isn't this what Jesus is saying when he says pray for those who despitefully use you? He is not thinking only of those people who despitefully use us, but he is thinking of the happiness that such praying can bring to the one who does the praying.

Recently in a town in Texas, I stated that "the best way to get rid of your enemies is to pray for them. It will help them and it will help you." After the service, I went back to the hotel and was fast asleep when the telephone rang. When I answered it, I heard a sob and then a woman's very tearful voice said, "Dr. Angell, I just can't do that." I asked gently, "Do what?" She answered, "I can't pray for someone that has used me despitefully. I can't do it and I'm miserable." The telephone clicked and the conversation was over. I never knew who she was nor what the situation was. This I do know—if you can't pray for people who despitefully use you, you *are* going to be miserable.

Another incident in my life presents the other side. When I was seventeen I went to work in a railroad machine shop. I was assigned to work with a most ungodly man. One day we had a tough job high up on a big engine. Nothing went right. The machinist was easily angered and ripped out oath after oath. Working close to us was Matt Duvall, the only Negro who was ever allowed to work in the beautiful spic-and-span white machine shop. He was affectionately known to all of us as Uncle Matt, and was one of the best Christians I have ever known. After one violent outburst of cursing, we looked down from the engine to see Uncle Matt standing on the floor below us with his hat off. Tearfully he said, in a most respectful voice, "Boss, please don't take my Lord's name in vain. It hurts me deep inside."

The machinist said in a rough voice, "Tend to your own business."

As Uncle Matt slowly turned to walk away he said, "I'se gwine pray for you."

For a while the machinist just sat still, then he mumbled something that I could not understand. But I did notice that whenever he cursed again, he looked to see if Uncle Matt was around. On that same job, the machinist had a terrible accident. A powerful electric drill jumped out of its place and caught in his overalls. It tore him all to pieces. He was taken to the nearby railroad hospital. When I visited him at the noon hour, I asked if there was anything I could do. He answered: "Just one thing. Ask Uncle Matt to pray for me." Prayer does change things as truly as it changes the one who prays.

III

That ye may be the children of your Father which is in heaven (Matt. 5:45).—Is Jesus saying, "Turn the other cheek, go the second mile, give to him that asketh thee; from him that would borrow from thee, turn not thou away; pray for them that despitefully use you and ye will be the children of your Father which is in heaven"? Is he saying, Do all of these things and they will make you become children of your Father which is in heaven? No. Then what does he mean? Isn't it this? If you do these things, people will know that you belong to God and he belongs to you. They will know that you couldn't possibly do these things without being a Christian—a child of God.

In the book, *Her Father's Daughter*, by Jean Stratton Porter, the father was a naturalist and loved all of the wild things that lived in the forest. The snakes never bit him, they never even coiled as he passed. No danger ever phased him. Even the squirrels did not hide, they just sat and looked at him. People marveled. The naturalist had one daughter who traveled with him constantly. When he died, she took his place. The wild things treated her just as they had her father and people said, "She is her father's daughter."

Just so, when you live like Jesus lived and do the things he challenged you to do, people will say, "She is the daughter of her Father in heaven," or "He is the son of his Heavenly Father."

S. H. Hadley in Jerry McAuley's Bowery mission related this incident:

"One night I gave the invitation at the midnight service, for all those who wanted to become Christians or wanted me to pray with them, to come and kneel at the altar. Down the aisle there came a bum whom I had seen often in the community. When he knelt to pray, I knelt by him. He was already praying and his prayer consisted of just one sentence which he repeated over and over, 'Dear Lord, make me like Joe.'

"I interrupted him to say, 'Ask God to make you like Jesus.'

"He opened his eyes and looked at me a moment in astonishment, then asked, 'Was Jesus any better than Joe?' Everybody on the Bowery loved Joe. He had been converted and had dedicated his life entirely to his Lord two years before. Only the Master knows how many men Joe led to Christ and sent them off the Bowery. We had buried Joe that afternoon and the bums of the Bowery wept."

I think this is what Jesus meant when he said, "Do these things and all the world will know that you are a child of God."

3
Is It Well with Thee?

Among the many students who attended Paul Meigs' church near Stanford University were two Chinese boys from the same hometown. Their families were immensely wealthy. Besides their actual expenses the boys each had three thousand dollars' spending money annually. So attentive were they that one day Dr. Meigs invited them to his study. Many were their questions about Christianity and the Bible. They became deeply concerned about their souls and weeks later accepted Christ as their Saviour and were baptized.

They shared with Dr. Meigs the burden they had for their parents and families who had never even heard about Christ and, of course, were not saved. How could they be told and how could they be convinced that the Christian God was *the* God, and that only through Christ could their sins be forgiven? After long hours of thinking and praying they worked out a plan. One of them was not on the Communist black list so he would write a letter to his father, tell him what had happened, and beg permission to fly home and talk to all of them about his newly found happiness. He wrote the letter, never mentioning his friend. The answer was short and heartbreaking: "We do not know you. Your name has been erased from our family record. Never write us again. Never come home again. You are disinherited. You are dead."

On reading that letter Dr. Meigs asked: "Does that mean you cannot finish college? How will you support yourself?" Then he commented, "What a pity!"

After a long silence, the other student said, "You don't understand, Doctor. That is not the problem. Our concern is that they are lost and he can never talk to them about Christ. But they don't know about me, so I'm going home to try to lead both my family and his to be Christians."

"But you are on the Communist black list. They will kill you."

He answered, "Yes, I know, but they won't do anything to me for a few months. First they will be all smiles, until they find they can't brainwash me. Then they will stand me up against a wall and let the firing squad shoot me. But I'll have those few months to try to lead my father and mother and my family to Christ. And I'm going to try to lead my friend's parents to accept my Saviour. We want you to pray for me. We believe God will answer our prayers."

As Dr. Meigs related this incident, he concluded. "God doesn't ask all of us to pay a price like that in order to witness for him. Are we even half as concerned about the spiritual welfare of our loved ones?"

It was then I remembered an Old Testament story I had not thought of for years—the story of Elisha and the Shunammite woman. As the woman came hurrying across the parched, hot sand to Elisha, he asked, "Is it well with thee? is it well with thy husband? is it well with the child?"

You recall the story. It is told in the fourth chapter of 2 Kings. God had Elisha prophesy that this Shunammite father and mother would be given a child, even though they were well advanced in years. The child, like Abraham's, was the most precious thing on earth to them. "When the child was grown, it fell on a day, that he went out to his father to the reapers. And he said unto his father, My head, my head. And he said to a lad, Carry him to his mother. And when he had taken him, and brought him to his mother, he sat on her knees till noon, and then died. And she went up, and laid him on the bed of the man of God, and shut the door upon him, and went out" (vv. 18–21). Then she called to her husband to saddle one of the donkeys, for she must go to "the man of God." When Elisha saw her coming, riding as fast as the burro could run, he sent Gehazi to hurry to meet her, and ask these questions: "Is it well with thee? is it well with thy husband? is it well with the child?" (v. 26).

These are questions we would do well to ask—and answer, even when there is no crisis. We may find, even as Dr. Meigs's two Chinese boys found, that it *is not well* with some who are dear to our hearts.

I

Is it well with thy home?— Elisha is asking, Is it well with all of those who are dear to you? Are their names all written in God's "book of remembrance" (Mal. 3:16)? "Heavenly places" is a phrase often found in the Bible. This is a beautiful description of what our Heavenly Father wants our homes to be—"a little spot of heaven in an alien land."

One of our ambassadors to a foreign country recently said, "You have invited me to tell you about the duties of an ambassador. Let me begin by telling you first of the embassy, the place where we live. The embassy is a little spot of America set down in an alien land. On the walls we have pictures of George Washington, Abraham Lincoln, Robert E. Lee, Stonewall Jackson, and the President of the United States, with a big flag—Old Glory—high over everything. When we had prohibition in the United States we had prohibition in the embassy. Inside the embassy the laws of *our own country* are supreme. We celebrate Christmas, Thanksgiving, and the Fourth of July. Outside, it is different. They celebrate none of these. Let me repeat, the embassy is a little spot of America in an alien land."

I never heard the balance of his speech. Racing through my mind was the thought that Christian homes should be "a little spot of heaven in an alien land." Our first reponsibility is to our Lord. The atmosphere should be filled with love and kindness. The spirit of Christ should leaven our thinking and our actions. Only then will it "be well with our homes."

The children in our homes are so sensitive and impressionable. They can "feel" our attitudes. Sometimes they surprise us with their power of discernment. The story is told of a mother who said: "My husband and I met each other in church and fell in love. We were married in church, and when our first boy was born we took him with us and put him in the Nursery. When he was old enough to walk, my husband and he went hand in hand to Sunday school. As the other children came along we found it easier just to drop him at Sunday school and go pick him up afterwards.

"One Sunday morning at the breakfast table, when he was about seven years old, he was so still and silent that I looked over the Sunday paper to see why. He had stopped eating and was staring into space. His eyes were not focused on anything. I touched my husband with my foot under the table and nodded toward the boy. After a moment my husband said, 'Son, what are you thinking so hard about?' His answer jarred us both. 'Daddy, don't you love Jesus any more?'

" 'Of course, I do. Why do you ask?'

" 'Well, my teacher said that if we loved Jesus we would do

what he wanted us to do, and he wants us to come to Sunday school and go to worship services. Daddy, you used to take me to Sunday school and I was so proud of you. Everybody liked you and smiled and shook hands with you and with me, too. I was happy all over.'

"The tears were close to dropping out of his eyes when my husband pushed his chair back and said huskily to the boy, 'Give me five minutes and I'll be ready and we'll walk into that Sunday school together, not just today but for always.'"

One day I spoke to a group of students at the University of Tennessee on the subject, "This is my Father's World." I put the emphasis on the word "Father." I had talked about God as a loving Father who knew and supplied all our wants and needs. I pictured him as one who knew our foibles and understood our weaknesses and yet loved us just the same. After the service, a young lady waited until the others had gone. I was shocked at her question, "Can't you find some better word for God than *Father?* It leaves me cold. My father was a brute. He was cruel and mean. My home is a miserable place because of him." As she walked away her pastor, who had heard it all, said, "Don't feel too bad about it, her life has been warped. Maybe nothing can ever get rid of the scars. The damage has been done. Her home, before it broke up, must have been a little spot of hell."

My mind went back to something I had just read. Scott Fitzgerald, famous novelist of our day, had just died and on his desk was found a plot for a new novel. He was going to write a book in which a wealthy man died and left a strange will. The will bequeathed all of his millions to be divided equally, share and share alike, to all of his relatives. There was one condition. They were to come and live together in his spacious mansion. Below the outlined plot was a note, "This could be a little spot of hell."

Stop a minute and think. Is it well with your home? Is it well with each loved one in your home? Is it well with your child?

A church bulletin that recently came to my desk tells a modern fable. "Once there was a little boy. When he was three weeks old his parents turned him over to a baby-sitter. When he was two they dressed him up like a cowboy and gave him a gun. When he was three everybody said, 'How cute!' as he went about lisping a beer commercial jingle. When he was six his father dropped him off at Sunday school. When he was eight they bought him a BB gun and taught him to shoot sparrows. He learned to shoot windshields by himself. When he was ten, he spent his afternoons at the drugstore newsstand reading comic books. His mother wasn't home and his father was busy. When he was thirteen, he told his parents other boys stayed out as late as they wanted to, so they said he could, too. It was easier that way. When he was fourteen they gave him a deadly two-ton machine, wrangled a license for him to drive it, and told him to 'be careful.' When he was fifteen, the police called his home one night and said, 'We have your boy. He's in trouble.' Screamed the father, 'It can't be MY boy!' But . . . it was."

II

Is it well with thy husband—wife?—Some years ago in a morning revival service I related the story of Thomas Carlyle:

He had married his secretary, who for many years continued working with him in his prolific writings. He was so absorbed that he let her continue working for several weeks after she became ill. The cancer was one of the slow growing ones. Finally, she was confined to her bed. Carlyle loved her but never found time to stay with her very long. When the end came and they took her to the cemetery, it was a rainy day and the mud was deep. After the funeral, Carlyle went back to his home badly shaken. He climbed the stairs to her room and sat down in a chair next to her bed, realizing he had not spent enough time with her in her illness. Carlyle picked up her diary from a bedside table and started to glance through it. Suddenly he became very alert, for on one page she had written a single line, "Yesterday he spent an hour with me and it was like being in heaven; I love him so." He turned to the next page. It nearly broke his heart, for there was written, "I have listened all day to hear his steps in the hall, but now it is late and I guess he won't come today." Carlyle read on through another half-dozen pages, then threw the book down and rushed back to the cemetery through the rain. His friends found him face down in the mud on the newly made grave. He was weeping and repeating over and over, "If I had only known, if I had only known."

After the service, a lady came up and asked, "Won't you please tell that same story in your sermon tonight? It is the story of my life. My husband is the sweetest and the best man I have ever known. He owns a big drugstore and gets up early to open it and stays late at night to close it. Our two boys never see him except at work. I take them down quite often in the afternoon just to be near him."

I told her I would be glad to repeat the story and preface it with the remark that someone in the morning congregation had requested me to repeat it. Quickly she answered, "That won't do, for he would know it was I. He has promised to come to church with me just this one night."

I thought a minute and said, "All right, I will tell it tonight, just like I forgot I had told it this morning."

I told the story that night without any explanation. After the service, when everybody except the woman, her husband,

and two boys had gone, I went back and sat down in front of them. I noticed traces of tears on the husband's face. Finally he blurted out, "I am just as guilty as Carlyle was, only I have found it out in time. From now on it is going to be different." Very beautifully he lived up to his promise, and Christmas after Christmas he sent me a big box of candy, along with a letter telling me that all was well.

III

Is it well with thee?—James L. Kraft, of Kraft cheese fame, spent the last few winters of his life in the Florida Everglades. Many Sundays he worshiped in the church I served in Miami. We were delighted to have him, for we knew his consecration and his partnership with God. One December morning I invited him to come up on the pulpit with me and say a word to our people. He begged off, and with a smile said, "If you want me to, I will preach for you next Sunday."

The next Sunday the ushers had to put chairs in the aisles to take care of the crowd. Mr. Kraft was at his best. He concluded his sermon with this experience:

"I was going to San Francisco to address a convention and the newspaper in my city had made a note of the fact. The night before I left, the telephone rang and a woman's voice with a lot of sadness in it said, 'Mr. Kraft, I see by the paper that you are going to San Francisco tomorrow and I want to ask a favor. My boy is in Alcatraz for life. I write him, send him money and boxes of cakes, candy, and cigarettes. I guess he gets them but he never writes me. Please go to see him and tell him I love him, and ask him to write to me just a note.'

"I promised her I would see the boy. A few days later I sat in the office of the warden and we talked for awhile, because we were old friends. Finally he said, 'Mr. Kraft, don't hurry but the boy you want to see is in the visitors' room. Just go down that steel enclosed corridor and the guards stationed along it will show you the way.'

"I went down the corridor to where it turned at right angles. Just as I made the turn, a big hand shot out in front of me and clamped me by the chest and a voice said, 'Stand perfectly still, Mr. Kraft, don't move for a moment.'

"I heard a faint buzzing sound and then the big policeman smiled and said, 'You can go on, Mr. Kraft, you are clean.'

"Irritated, I answered him roughly, 'I'm always clean.'

"He just smiled indulgently and said, 'I mean you don't have anything in your pockets which you ought not to take into the visitors' room. I just looked through your pockets.'

"Not believing him, I said, 'Just what do I have in my pockets?'

"Still smiling, he enumerated: 'Your car keys in your right trousers pocket, some change and a little pen knife in your left trousers pocket, and metal glasses case in your inside pocket.'

"I left him and went on down the corridor. Just before I reached the next bend, the thought struck me suddenly. Suppose that when I turn the next corner Christ should put out his hand and stop me and say, 'Stand still a minute, Mr. Kraft, and let me see if you are clean *inside*.' I stopped right where I was, took off my hat, bowed my head, and asked God to search my heart and see if I was clean inside."

His closing prayer was: "Lord, when I stand before thee in the great day of the judgment, I want above everything else to hear you say, 'This is my beloved son, in whom I am well pleased.'"

Every one of us should get down on our knees and ask the Lord to search our hearts and answer the question that Elisha asked the Shunammite woman, "Is it well with thee?"

4
Overtones of the Twenty-third Psalm

As I parked my car in front of a big city hospital in Miami, one of our best-loved physicians came down the steps and started toward his car. It happened that it was very near mine, so, I waited. When he came close, I noticed that his lips were moving as though he were talking. With a grin, I said, "Bascom, you are too young to be talking to yourself."

He smiled, "I wasn't talking to myself. I was saying the twenty-third Psalm." Maybe the expression of surprise and delight on my face made him continue. "I just came from the room of a little old saint on the fourth floor who can't live much longer. She asked me if I knew the twenty-third Psalm. When I told her I claimed that psalm as my very own and that I leaned on it every day, she replied, 'Let's say it together.'"

His voice was a little husky when he asked, "Didn't Jesus call himself the Good Shepherd? Wasn't he talking about himself when he pictured the shepherd's going into the mountains after that one sheep that didn't come in?" Then very slowly he quoted the first few verses, "The Lord is my shepherd; I shall not want. He maketh me to lie down in green pastures: he leadeth me beside the still waters. He restoreth

31

my soul." Thoughtfully, he added, "This twenty-third Psalm has been enshrined on a marble pedestal too long. We need to take it down and break it up and use it. It's something to live with and live by."

Maybe he was right. Certainly each verse or "piece," as the doctor called it, contains a valuable and usable and needed message. But I like to think of each sentence as a musical instrument in a divine orchestra. The symphony would be incomplete if any one were missing. Read the psalm thoughtfully, then lay the Bible down and listen. The overtones bring a sense of security and a peace of mind. Look closely at some of the "pieces" which contribute so much to the "overtones."

I

The Lord is my shepherd.—When David wrote these words for and about his God, he was paying him the most beautiful compliment. David was a shepherd. He knew the responsibilities, and he knew the sacrifices a shepherd must make. He was the flock's protection from the predatory beasts of the forest. When he wrote, "Thou preparest a table before me in the presence of mine enemies," wasn't he picturing himself, standing between his feeding flock and the deep, dark woods which might be a hiding place for ravenous wolves?

The needs of his flock formed a big part of David's responsibility. Jesus called himself the "Good Shepherd." One day to the multitude he spoke these comforting words, "Come unto me, all ye that labour and are heavy laden, and I will give you rest" (Matt. 11:28).

Kate Smith, of radio fame, illustrates so beautifully the words of that old song, "His eye is on the sparrow, and I know He cares for me."

"When I was ten years old, my family went down for a vacation to Colonial Beach on the Potomac, close to where it flows into the Chesapeake Bay. Two little girls, who lived in the cottage close by, and I became fast friends. One day they invited me to go out in their canoe. It was a beautiful, calm, lovely day. The water was as smooth as glass, and the sun was warm and bright. We paddled and drifted out into the Potomac. We were so engrossed in our conversation that we didn't notice that the skies were becoming leaden and overclouded, and the wind had come up. Suddenly, we realized we were a long way from shore and we started paddling. Then, without any warning, the canoe flipped over.

"Crying and screaming, we hung onto the canoe. Then I started praying. I said, 'O God, my mamma told me you were never too busy with the big things to listen when a little girl needed some help. O God, please listen now. Send *somebody*, send *somebody*.' "Up out of the breaking waves and the misty Chesapeake there came a fishing boat. Its nose turned toward us and a big man reached over and hauled us aboard. He pulled our canoe out and laid it across the bow of his boat and took us all to shore. From that day on I have worshiped a God who had time to listen to anything I had to say, had time to consider any need that I had.

"As the years have rolled along, I have realized that God needed that fishing boat that day, and that maybe God needs me as an undershepherd. So, every time I've seen a task that I thought God needed me to do I've tried to do it. The greatest joy of my life has come out of being one of his undershepherds.

"Back in 1936, when the Ohio River flooded the country around it and thousands of people were in need, I turned my life over to God to help out. Along toward Christmas, when some of them were still without homes and I was still helping, I received a pitiful letter from a little girl saying, 'I wish so much Santa Claus would bring me a doll for Christmas, but

Mamma tells me Santa Claus can't come to us this year. But I still believe he can find a way, and I thought I'd write and tell you, for maybe he would hear your radio broadcast. If you think he can, please ask him to bring me a doll.'

"I read that letter over the radio, and I said, 'Some of you who want to help Santa Claus out, send this little girl a doll.' The answers to that broadcast request made me weep. More than eight thousand dolls came in addressed to that little girl. I looked at that great stack of packages and the letters that came along with the checks, and I realized that across this America of ours there were a lot of people who believed in God and believed in being undershepherds for this God of ours. I couldn't help but think that the leaven of Christianity has gotten into the hearts and homes of Americans *far* better than we have any idea."

"The Lord is my shepherd, I shall not want." Do you believe in God? Do you believe in a God that will supply your needs in life? Then you *have* to believe in a God that will want you to help supply the needs of others. It's a grand commission. It has lots of happiness, contentment, fun, peace, adventure, and living tied up in it.

I love that old song that says, "If you want me, you can find me, I'll be somewhere a-workin' for my Lord; If you call me, I will answer, I'll be somewhere a-workin' for my Lord."

II

He maketh me to lie down in green pastures—Recently, I was riding home from a funeral with one of our consecrated elderly deacons. In the service I had read this beloved twenty-third Psalm, and we were talking about its beauty, when he said, "I heard an old minister preach a sermon on 'Green Pastures' once, and the thought he presented was new to me. It has been a blessing to my life ever since. He said there was just one reason the shepherd had for timing his direction so that the sheep would be in deep grass at the noonday rest period. They would be well fed and content to lie down. Also, they would know that a feast awaited them when they awoke. It would give them a sense of security."

Immediately, I thought of that crowd of Korean children whose parents had been killed or captured. Our Red Cross gathered a group of them into an improvised hospital, fed and clothed them, but at night they were restless and couldn't sleep. A psychiatrist was called in and after watching them through a night, said, "Feed them well at supper and then when you put them to bed, give each one a slice of bread to hold in his hand. Tell them it is theirs to eat when morning comes." A night nurse said, "It would almost make you cry to see them grow restless, then awake in the night, look at the bread, sometimes taste it, then hide it under the covers and go back to sleep."

I think there is another reason that God makes us lie down in green pastures. The green pastures are so tempting that we don't want to stop and be still for a moment. We get too busy accumulating earthly things. We rush through life so fast we forget to "be still and know that I am God." Jesus asked a question once—a question that none of us should forget for a single day. "For what is a man profited, if he shall gain the whole world, and lose his own soul? or what shall a man give in exchange for his soul" (Matt. 16:26)?

A fellow pastor walked into the busy office of one of his deacons not long ago. Everybody was in a mad rush. The man he had come to see owned the company. As the pastor walked in, three men bustled out. Before he could say a word, a clerk rushed in and shoved a paper in front of the man to sign, then jerked it away and rushed out. Everybody seemed to be in double-quick time. The typewriters clattered, the doors banged. It was a madhouse. The pastor said he sat there for two or three minutes before his friend looked up and asked, 'What's on your mind, Preacher?" Then he went back to writing again.

The pastor said, "I just sat still. Then I did a thing that shocked him speechless. In a very low, slow voice I quoted:

Let-not-your-heart-be-troubled. Neither-let-it-be-afraid. In-my-Father's-house-are-many-mansions. If-it-were-not-so-I-would-have-told-you. Come-unto-me-all-ye-that-are-weary-and-heavy-laden-and-I-will-give-you-rest. The-Lord-is-my-Shepherd-I-shall-not-want. He-maketh-me-to-lie-down-in-green-pastures. He-lead-eth-me-beside-the-still-waters. He-restoreth-my-soul.

"I quoted on a little while and my friend's face relaxed and he leaned back in his chair. An expression like a little boy who needed his mother came over his face. When I got up and started toward the door he said, 'Preacher, come back again and do it all over.' "

We need to be still—to lie down in green pastures.

III

He leadeth me beside the still waters.—We know that sheep will not drink out of a rushing, turbulent stream. We *should* know that we, too, need to be refreshed by spending some time in a quiet place. Noise can shatter glasses. It can also shatter our nervous systems. Noise can kill. So the phrase "beside the still waters" contributes beautifully to the sooth-ing overtones of this grand old psalm. Jesus scolded the Phari-sees for doing *even good things* and leaving the "inside of the cup" unclean. He called them "whited sepulchers," because they were washing the outside of the cup and neglecting the inside. They spent their time trying to impress *people* with their piety. They sought the most public place in which to pray. It is hard to picture a Pharisee's kneeling "beside the still waters" or asking God to wash his soul clean. Jesus said, "Blessed are the meek: for they shall inherit the earth. Blessed are they which do hunger and thirst after righteousness: for they shall be filled" (Matt. 5:5–6).

Six places in the Gospels we are told that Jesus went "apart to pray." Ten thousand times more we need to go "apart to pray" in some quiet place "beside the still waters." We need to let our Heavenly Father wash clean our minds and remove the alloy that can spoil our lives. Let me illustrate.

A physicist was showing his class an experiment. He had a bottle, a nail, and a piece of board. He took the nail and drove it into the board, using the bottle as a hammer. Then holding the bottle up, he said, "This is the hardest glass that's made. You saw me hit the nail hard blows with it; but there is no chip, no break." Then he said, "Watch."

He reached over and picked up a little piece of carborundum, the heaviest metal made, and dropped it into the bottle. He stepped back, shielded his face with his left hand, and struck the nail a light blow. The bottle flew into a hundred pieces. He said, "If I were a preacher, I'd take these things into the pulpit. I'd take a little piece of carborundum, a bottle, a nail, and a board, and when everybody was sufficiently curious and surprised, I'd say to them, 'You can buck all of the tough winds of life and travel the hard roads of life until you get something inside of you that doesn't belong there. It might be any of a multitude of things—hatred, resentment, or any other sin which causes you to break all to pieces. Then I would illustrate with the experiment you just witnessed."

Each sentence of this beautiful psalm is a priceless gem. Read each slowly, thoughtfully, and then listen to the overtones. To me they bring an assurance of security and "a peace that passeth understanding."

5
The Master's Call

The miracles of Jesus fall roughly into two groups—compassion and purpose. The word "compassion" comes from two words which, translated, mean suffer and with. Most of the miracles are in this group. They accent the tenderness of the Master. Of course, they are in a way purposeful miracles, too, for Jesus came to reveal his Heavenly Father as a God who loves us and cares.

A beautiful example is the story of the healing of the woman "bent with an infirmity." Jesus was teaching in a synagogue one sabbath day, when he saw this crippled woman. He called her to him and made her straight (cf. Luke 13:11). He "suffered with" every sufferer. Remember the hungry thousands who had come a long distance to see him and listen to his teaching? It was late in the evening when his disciples entreated him to dismiss them and let them go home for they were tired and hungry. (According to Matthew's account, he looked on them with *compassion* and told his disciples to feed them.) The disciples were astounded, *all but one*. One of his inner circle seems to have learned the lesson that Jesus had been trying so hard to teach all of them.

Andrew said, "There is a lad here, which hath five barley loaves, and two small fishes." I imagine Jesus looked on him and loved him as he replied: "Make the men sit down. . . . So the men sat down, in number about five thousand" (John 6:9–10). Then Jesus returned thanks over the lad's lunch and fed the multitude.

The outstanding example in the group of "planned miracles" or miracles of "purpose" is the raising of Lazarus. Once again we find a beautiful intermingling of "purpose" and "compassion," for in this story, set in a verse by itself, we read that "Jesus wept" (John 11:35). This miracle stands alone. It never ended with the resurrection of Lazarus. Maybe it hasn't ended yet. It sealed the death warrant for Jesus. Was this also part of its purpose? Who knows? John's record reads, "Then from that day forth they took counsel together for to put him to death" (11:53). But that wasn't the end either.

Look again at the story and some of the truths it contains. You will recall that a messenger was sent one day to Jesus to tell him that Lazarus, "whom Jesus loved," was sick. Since Lazarus and his two sisters, Mary and Martha, were so dear to him, you would naturally think that Jesus would have come with all haste. Certainly Mary and Martha, Lazarus' sisters, expected him to come immediately. But Jesus tarried.

When he arrived at Bethany, Martha greeted him with what seems to be a mild rebuke, "If thou hadst been here, my brother had not died" (v. 21). Mary also blamed him for not coming sooner (cf. v. 32). While it was hard for them to understand, I think it is relatively easy for us. This miracle laid the foundation for three wonderful triumphs that followed.

Lazarus and Martha and Mary had a host of friends in Jerusalem. John tells us that the crowds came to comfort and console the sisters. They were there when Jesus raised Lazarus, who had been in the tomb for four days. This was exciting news, and they rushed back to Jerusalem to spread it over the city. Who were the thousands that came out to meet him and spread their cloaks and palm fronds for the little donkey, that Jesus rode, to walk upon? Why did they do this? Most certainly this miracle was partly responsible.

The disciples of Jesus needed to see an empty tomb. They needed to see a resurrection. John spells it out for us. Jesus told his little band of followers, before the miracle, "Lazarus is dead. . . . *I am glad for your sakes that I was not there, to the intent ye may believe;* nevertheless let us go unto him" (11:14–15). Though they had been with him for three years they yet were not ready for the crucifixion and resurrection. He said to them, "This sickness is not unto death, *but for the glory of God, that the Son of God* might be glorified thereby" (v. 4). Through this miracle Jesus prepared them for another empty tomb, resurrection, and triumph.

It paved the way for the Pentecostal revival. Who were the thousands who listened to Simon Peter on that memorable day when he fearlessly told them that they had crucified the Son of God—the Prince of peace? They cried out in anguish, "What shall we do?" Their ears were wide open when the unlettered Galilean told them to repent and believe. Would there have been a Pentecostal revival without this miracle? Would they have accepted the empty tomb had there not been an empty tomb at Bethany?

There is another question that comes to every thinking person who reads this story in John's Gospel. Wasn't it cruel of Jesus to let Lazarus and his sisters suffer? The answer ought to strengthen us. Sometimes God needs to let someone suffer in order that his kingdom might come into the hearts of others. Many of us must belong to the "Fellowship of Scars," if his "kingdom is to come, and his will be done on earth as it is in heaven." The disciples suffered. Tradition has it that they were all martyrs, but they were not all of the martyrs. Paul, Knox, and many others belong to the "Fellowship of Scars."

Not long ago a missionary had come home from darkest Africa to bring three of her children that they might go to school in America. After she had found homes for them, through the help of our Woman's Missionary Union, and all arrangements had been made for their care, she made her reservations to return to Africa. The evening before she left, a group of fine Christian people gave her a farewell reception. One of them said to her, "I am sure you are anxious to get back to your mission field."

For a moment there was a frown on the missionary's face and then very solemnly she answered, "No, I am not anxious to get back. The place to which I am going is dirty. There are no electric lights, there are no modern conveniences whatsoever. There is no pure water, and I will be cooking on my wood stove, and while I cook I will be weeping because my children are so far away. I will be desperately lonesome for them and wondering if any of them is sick. When I remember that it will be three years before I see them again, I will be tempted to tell the Lord that I can't stand it and I am going home. No, I'm not anxious to get back, but I am more anxious to do the Lord's will than to do anything else. I would be more miserable here than there." She, too, belongs to the "Fellowship of Scars."

Now, look at these words that Martha spoke to Mary, "The Master is come, and calleth for thee," and remember that the Master still comes and still calls—for you and me.

I

He comes to restore happiness.—This he certainly did to his beloved friends Mary, Martha, and Lazarus. David wrote in the twenty-third Psalm, "He restoreth my soul." That is the way it reads in the King James Version. Another translation reads, "He refreshes and restores my life" (The Amplified Old Testament). Christ said once, and implied often, that he came that we might have life and have it more abundantly.

Follow Jesus across the three short years of his life and note how many times he restored happiness to miserable people. His was a beautiful "ministry of restoration." Is there a single miracle that did not *restore* joy to one or many people? His very first miracle relieved the misery and embarrassment of the host at the feast in Cana of Galilee. The supply of wine was not sufficient, and we can imagine the mental anguish of the man who made the feast when he realized the predicament. The whole family would have "lost face" forever. I am sure their gratitude lasted the rest of their lives, for the stillness and misery of the hour turned to gaiety and laughter, because Jesus was there. From that day to the end of his earthly life, Jesus went about restoring happiness to the blind, the lame, the lepers, and the sick who came to him.

So, he comes and calls for us, even as he did in the "days of old," to lift us out of the dungeons of despair, to put smiles on our faces and songs in our hearts. Let me illustrate. On the first day Joseph Fort Newton preached in his new pastorate in London, he said, "I was waiting in the pastor's study the last few minutes before the morning service. I was homesick. I was tense. I was in a strange church and a strange country. I was afraid they wouldn't like my American accent. I kept saying to myself, 'Why, oh, why did I accept this call?'" When there came a gentle knock at the door, I opened it and looked into the smiling face of the chairman of the deacon board. He came in carrying a huge basket of red roses. He set them down and said, 'Doctor, at prayer meeting last Wednesday night we spent the whole hour in prayer for you. All of us realized you were coming into a strange place and that you might be nervous and maybe homesick. So, everybody made a contribution to buy you a basket of roses and told me to tell you that every one of them would be present this morning. Also, that they would be praying for you, and when you looked over the congregation and your glance met theirs, they would smile at you so you would recognize them.' When I started to speak, he held up his hand, shook his head, and tipped out. He closed the door softly and I was alone again. No, I wasn't alone any more. The Master's presence filled the room. All of the fear and tension and nervousness were gone. I was among God's people and he was here."

II

He comes because we need him to save our very lives.—As the Bible tells us, "All we like sheep have gone astray." The people of Jesus' day looked for a Saviour. But the Saviour they expected in their minds was limited to one who would break the Roman yoke and save their nation and their dignity. Jesus does save people—physically, morally, and spiritually.

One night Charles Haddon Spurgeon preached about one sheep that didn't come in and the shepherd who went out to find it. After the service, a stranger said, "Dr. Spurgeon, I wish I had known you were going to preach on that story. I could have given you a wonderful illustration. I'm a hunter and not long ago I went with a guide to hunt in the mountains of Scotland. We stopped for lunch on a little plateau that was surrounded by high mountains and high grassy plains. I picked up my binoculars and searched the mountains around us. On one of them there was a sheep far below the top of another high plateau. I handed my binoculars to my guide and said, 'Look, how will he ever get back?' The wise old guide, who had spent his life in those mountains, said sadly, 'He can't get back *alone*. He has left the flock and unnoticed by the shepherd has jumped down to a grassy ledge. After he ate the grass on that ledge he jumped down to the one below. Unless the shepherd finds him quickly and helps him back he is lost, for the eagles have already seen him and are circling above him. One of them will come down screaming and flapping his wings, and the scared sheep will fall off the ledge.' We watched for a half hour and then the prophecy of my guide came true. It was a heartbreaking scene." Dr. Spurgeon, in writing about the parable of the lost sheep, said, "It is a perfect illustration that, unless the Master finds us and saves us, we will be lost—not just physically but for eternity."

III

The Master comes and calls because he needs us.—In many of the miracles that Jesus performed he needed a *third* person. In this miracle he stood before the rock cave in which the body of Lazarus had been placed and said to those about him, "Take ye away the stone." When he fed the five thousand he needed a little boy's lunch and he needed his disciples to carry the food to the waiting people. When blind Bartimaeus called to him, "Jesus, thou son of David, have mercy on me" (Mark 10:47), he needed someone to lead Bartimaeus to him. When he healed the man of the palsy he needed four men to carry the sick man from his home, tear up the roof, and lower the litter down to his feet. When he wanted to identify himself to his disciples after his resurrection, he needed those old fishermen to lower the net on the "other side of the boat."

Again, the end is not yet, for he needs us to help him to take the message of salvation to others who are lost. May God forgive us for our negligence. I wish I knew to whom I am indebted for the best illustration of this I ever heard. It read about like this: "In a dream I was in a crowded courtroom. The judge was already on the bench. I was being tried for my life and my lawyer and I sat at a table reserved for us. He was very nervous and kept watching the door. A half-dozen times he said, 'If I just had that one witness.'

"Finally, the judge rapped with his gavel and asked if we were prepared to begin. My attorney pleaded for another five minutes and said, 'There is one important witness that hasn't arrived.' Again he glanced at the door and wiped the perspiration from his forehead. Suddenly, the door burst open and a little fat man came down the aisle. He, too, was perspiring and mopping his face. The judge called the court into session and directed the little fat man to the witness chair. He apologized for being late and started a long, rambling speech about his new car. He said that he didn't know quite how to operate it, but that he planned to take his family on a vacation in it soon. Then he told the judge where they were going on their vacation. All the time I was squirming in my seat, and I said, half aloud, 'Why doesn't he shut up about his car and tell the judge what he could tell that would save my life,' for my life was at stake, and here he was wasting time telling about his new car and his vacation.

"Suddenly, I was wide awake, sitting up in bed with the perspiration streaming down *my* face. Immediately there flashed into my mind that only yesterday a new family had moved in next door to us, and my pastor had called to tell me that the mother and children were Christians, but that the husband was not. He wanted me to get acquainted with him and bring him to church. So, I did go over to the fence and we had a nice chat. Now, *I* am a little fat man, and I *had* talked to him about my new car and my vacation plans, but not once in all of our conversation did I say anything to him about my church or about my Saviour."

I repeat, Jesus often comes and calls us because he needs us to be his witnesses, his ambassadors—until the world ends.

6
Same Old World?

The phrase, "the same old world," belongs to Walter Pitkin, the man who wrote *Life Begins at Forty*. He said there were seven things he wanted to do again before he died. One of them was to spend a week watching the sunsets in the Everglades of Florida. I know what he meant, for they defy description. It is said they attain their beauty because the moisture and perfumed gases in the Everglades fill the atmosphere and the setting sun brings out all the colors of the rainbow. He calls it "God's unspoiled and untouched world." It was in this connection that he used the words the "same old world" that God created.

Not long ago I was sitting on the bow of a very fast boat, traveling at such speed that the front half of the boat did not even touch the water. Two of us had spent the day fishing in the Ten Thousand Islands which are a part of the Everglades. As we came around one island after another, we often faced the sunset. Suddenly the motor slowed down and the boat stopped. I said, "Bill, what's the matter?" Pointing to the sunset, he answered, "Let's sit here and watch it for a while. It's so much more beautiful than anything man ever made. I wonder if they have been like that ever since God created the world."

A passage from Ecclesiastes came back to me, "The sun also ariseth, and the sun goeth down, and hasteth to his place where he arose. The wind goeth toward the south, and turneth about unto the north; it whirleth about continually, and the wind returneth again according to his circuits" (1:5–6). Same old world. "All the rivers run into the sea; yet the sea is not full; unto the place from whence the rivers come, thither they return again. All things are full of labour; man cannot utter it: the eye is not satisfied with seeing, nor the ear filled with hearing. The thing that hath been, it is that which shall be; and that which is done is that which shall be done: and *there is no new thing under the sun*" (vv. 7–9). There is nothing new under the sun. It's the same old world.

Then the words of Paul flashed in my mind, "Therefore if any man be in Christ, *he is a new creature: old things are passed away; behold, all things are become new.* And all things are of God, who hath reconciled us to himself by Jesus Christ (2 Cor. 5:17–18).

I

There is a definite sense in which we live in the same old world.—Materials in this world change form, but scientists tell us the world is just as heavy and no heavier than when it was first created. They tell us that we can burn things up and change the form of them. They go into gas, smoke, flame, and heat, but, then, by and by they return again to become solids, even as Solomon said in Ecclesiastes. We build our houses out of wood and dust and dirt. We build them out of sand and clay, and we make our blocks out of rock and sand. If we leave them alone for a while and don't do anything to protect them from the hammers of God, the elements—sun, rain, wind, and change of climate—beat them back to dust. There *is* a sense in which it's the same old world—materially the same old world.

When I went to San Antonio to become pastor of the First Baptist Church, the state of Texas was repairing The Alamo. They had torn down one wall. The big oblong blocks were piled up awaiting some cement patching, for they were crumbling. They were full of bullet holes. I wanted one of the bullets for a souvenir, so I took my pocket knife and tried to dig one out. The long blade reached to the bottom of the hole, but all I found was a lump of dust. The steel bullet had disintegrated. I thought of the words I so often quote at funerals, "Earth to earth, ashes to ashes, dust to dust." The hammers of God, the elements, had done their work well.

There is another way in which it is the same old world. There was, is, and always will be a component element in all human life—adversity. For trouble is an inevitable part of human experience upon this planet and cannot be continually or totally evaded or avoided.

An ancient ruler called his prime minister into his presence and said, "I want you to write for me a history of the world." The prime minister summoned his consultants and framed a history of the world, making up five hundred volumes. He presented it to the sultan, saying, "I have here several hundred donkeys, and several hundred volumes containing the history of the world." The emperor looked at that mass of material and remarked, "Well, could it not be reduced to an amount of material that would be a readable portion?" The prime minister waited a bit and then replied, "Sire, it could be put all in one sentence. These volumes contain the life and experiences of men who have lived, who have suffered, and died."

One might think this a rather depressing summary of life, and yet it is an accurate one, a realistic one, an appropriate one. For surely, anybody who has observed life at all knows that trouble and adversity are as universal as human nature itself. It knocks at the door of every heart sooner or later. It knocks at the door of the wealthy and the poor—it is no respecter of persons. It comes to the aristocratic and the plebeian. It comes to the peasant; it comes to the philosopher. It comes to the believer; it comes to the unbeliever; and somewhere, sometime, misfortune, hardship, adversity will come. Same old world.

Also, there is a sense in which it is the same old world morally. As the same natural laws of gravitation work, so the same natural laws of the spiritual world work. They do not change. "Whatsoever a man soweth, that shall he also reap" (Gal. 6:7). It has always been and always will be that way. "Be sure your sin will find you out" (Num. 32:23). "Cast thy bread upon the waters: for thou shalt find it after many days" (Eccl. 11:1). Let me illustrate:

A farmer hurt the feelings of a fourteen-year-old boy who lived on the adjoining farm. The boy was so irritated that he could not sleep that night. He tried to think of some way he could get even. It was nearly dawn when an idea came to him. Early that morning he mounted his horse and rode twenty miles to purchase a bag of Johnson grass seed. After dark he sowed the richest bottom land that his neighbor owned with the seed. Now, if you are a farmer, you know you can fight Johnson grass most of your lifetime without killing it. So, the grass came up, and the neighbor fought Johnson grass until he died. In the meantime, the boy grew up and fell in love with the neighbor's daughter. They were married, and when the father died he left the farm to his daughter. The man who sowed the field said, "For a little over forty years I have fought Johnson grass."

You reap what you sow. Your sins find you out. You pay

for them. In the strangest ways, the payment comes back. We do not have to wait until this life is over.

Clovis Chappell and I recently participated in a series of "Preaching Missions." The last one was in Huntington, West Virginia. He gave me one of his latest books, titled *If I Were Young*. As I looked at the table of contents, I mused aloud at the title of chapter 7, "If I Were Young I'd Make People Treat Me Right." "Just how would you make people treat you right?" I turned the pages to the chapter and found the text. It was the Golden Rule. I sat thinking, "Yes, you could make people treat you right if you practiced the Golden Rule, if you practiced grace—giving to others that which they need, not that which they *deserve*." If you would live on that high spiritual plane people would treat you right, just as Clovis Chappell said, and just as Jesus said, "With what measure ye mete, it shall be measured to you" (Mark 4:24).

Usually when we preachers take for a text: "Whatsoever a man soweth, that shall he also reap" (Gal. 6:7), we slant it *down*. We preach about the wages of sin and the disasters that wrong living brings. We talk about "wild oats." I'm guilty of doing that very thing. But the other side is just as true and much more beautiful. When we sow good seed we reap glorious harvests. Let me illustrate:

In the city of Philadelphia there was a little third class hotel. Into it one night there came two tired elderly people. They went up to the night clerk and the husband pleadingly said, "Mister, please don't tell us you don't have a room. My wife and I have been all over the city looking for a place to stay. We did not know about the big conventions that are here. The hotels at which we usually stay are all full. We're dead tired and it's after midnight. Please don't tell us you don't have a place where we can sleep."

The clerk looked at them a long moment and then answered, "Well, I don't have a single room except my own. I work at night and sleep in the daytime. It's not as nice as the other rooms, but it's clean, and I'll be happy for you to be my guests for tonight."

The wife said, "God bless you, young man."

The next morning at the breakfast table, the couple sent the waiter to tell the night clerk they wanted to see him on very important business. The night clerk went in, recognized the two people, sat down at the table and said he hoped they had had a good night's sleep. They thanked him most sincerely. Then the husband astounded the clerk with this statement, "You are too fine a hotel man to stay in a hotel like this. How would you like for me to build a big, beautiful, luxurious hotel in the city of New York and make you general manager?"

The clerk didn't know what to say. He thought there might be something wrong with their minds. He finally stammered, "It sounds wonderful." His guest then introduced himself. "I'm John Jacob Astor." So, the Waldorf Astoria Hotel was built, and the night clerk became, in the years to follow, the best-known hotel man in the world.

Same old world? "Cast your bread upon the waters." It is the same old world, just exactly like the writer of Ecclesiastes said, "The winds *do* come out of the south, whirl around, go back and come out again. The sun *does* go down and then comes up again; and waters *do* go into the sea and the sea is not full, for the sun picks them up and wafts them back across the world, and they fall in refreshing showers, they run down the rivers into the sea, and the sea is never full." It is the same old world in many respects.

II

Likewise, there is an area in which we live in a new world.— When Paul says, "If any man be in Christ, he is a new creature: old things are passed away; behold, all things are become new" (2 Cor. 5:17), there is no conflict. He is not talking about changing the material world; he is talking about changing people. It is like Jesus said to Nicodemus, we can be born again. Our lives can be changed and made wonderful. All this world can become brand new. I *know* what he is talking about.

I remember the day, the Sunday, I walked down the aisle, with my heart up in my throat, and told the minister I wanted to be a Christian. I lived back in the mountains where there was a swinging bridge 'way up above the James River. I had watched it when there was a cloudburst on the head of the river, causing it to rise out of its banks and lap that swinging bridge. One of my pals stood on it, foolishly bouncing it up and down so that it touched the water. A tree came floating down, hit the bridge, and broke it into pieces. We found his body a week later, wedged between two rocks in the Iron Gate Gap. I had to cross that bridge often and I was afraid. My fear was intensified when I thought, "If this thing breaks, I won't go to heaven, I'll go straight to hell. I don't belong to God, I don't belong to Christ."

Then that Sunday came and I gave my life to Christ. On a Monday morning, I walked out on that bridge and deliberately made it swing. I was in a new world, I belonged to Christ, I belonged to God. I wasn't afraid of anything. It didn't matter if it did drop, heaven was a better place than this world. Those were my childish thoughts as I stood there. I lived in a *new* world.

Immediately following Paul's statement that all things are new, God had him write a challenge to us—to be ambassadors, God's ambassadors. We are to go out into the world and tell all people that God sent Christ down here to reconcile all of us to him, for all have sinned and like sheep have gone astray.

Christ can and will open the doors to a new world if we will let him. This commission to be ambassadors is a beautiful echo of the Great Commission, "Go ye into all the world, and preach the gospel to every creature" (Mark 16:15).

One of our prominent scholars has said the thought of that passage reads: "*As you go*, preach the gospel." Luke adds, "beginning at Jerusalem" (Luke 24:47). Many Christians have found it easier to *send* ambassadors to the distant parts of the world than to walk across the street and witness to a neighbor. The challenge of our Master is to *be* an ambassador, not just *send* one. So live that your life is a witness of the changing power of Christ.

While I was attending the University of Pennsylvania, I heard John Wanamaker speak a number of times. He has been called "The Merchant Prince" of Philadelphia. When he died, the editor of the Philadelphia *Inquirer* devoted the whole editorial page to him with a large picture in the center. He closed the editorial with this incident. It read about like this:

I was in John Wanamaker's Sunday school class. We didn't have any classrooms, so we met in the church auditorium. We boys used to get there early so we could sit close to him. The first two boys to get there sat down in the middle of the church, leaving room between them for John Wanamaker. And the next who came sat down on the pew behind him where they could touch him, or in front of him so they could turn and look up into his face. We loved him. He was our ideal. We all went to work for him when we got old enough to quit school. He gave me a job wrapping packages. After I'd been there awhile, I discovered a new way to wrap a package that I thought was neater, and certainly was faster. So, I just took a piece of paper, a string, and a shoe box and went up to John Wanamaker's office on the third floor. I was going to show him my discovery. When I got in front of that office door and saw all of those desks and all of those men and women in that big room, with John Wanamaker way in the back, his office door open, sitting behind a big mahogany desk, I lost my nerve. I went back downstairs. I couldn't do it.

The next day I tried it again, but I just couldn't go in. I said to myself, "Well, he's my Sunday school teacher. I can talk to him on Sunday." Sunday I got there early and told him what I had discovered about wrapping packages.

He asked, "Well, why didn't you come up to my office and show me? I'm always wanting to learn."

I said, "I tried, but I was afraid."

He said, "You're not afraid of *me*. Tomorrow morning at nine o'clock come to my office. That's an order."

Next morning at nine o'clock, I was there. He welcomed me with a smile, pushing his chair back so he could see a little better as I put the paper down on his big, beautiful desk. I put the package on it, wrapped it up quickly, tied it, and stepped back. Flinging my hands out with a flourish, I knocked his ink bottle over and the ink spread out all over his desk. I wanted the floor to open up and swallow me.

Mr. Wanamaker reached down, opened a drawer, still smiling, and took out a pack of blotters. He said, "Now, you showed me how to wrap up a package better than I ever saw it done before, and faster, too. I'm going to show you how to attack that sea of ink. Take half of these blotters and help me. Don't slap one down in the middle of the ink or it will splash all over everything. Creep up on it real easy with the edge of a blotter and I'll creep up on the other side. When you get your blotter full, drop it in the wastepaper basket." By and by, our blotters met in the middle of the desk and my Sunday school teacher was still smiling. *That day I gave my life to God.*

Ambassadors? Yes, we can be God's ambassadors with a consistent Christian life, with the things we do, the things we want to do. We can be his ambassadors with the attitudes we express, the words we say, the thoughts we think, and the plans we lay. We can be God's ambassadors with the examples that we live before other people. We can be his ambassadors to make all things new in the lives of others. His command is, "As you go, preach."

7
God's Jewel Case

Not long ago I made a special trip from a nearby city to Washington, D.C., just to see the Hope Diamond which was on display in the Smithsonian Institute. As many of you know, it is the most beautiful *blue* diamond in the world. There are no words with which to describe it. For a long time, I stood above it and looked through the bulletproof glass at it and its roommate, the Portuguese Diamond. The Portuguese Diamond is twice the size of the Hope Diamond and brilliantly white. There were four guards in the room. Finally, one of them walked over to me and I asked, "What is the value of these two jewels?" He answered, "No price has ever been put on the two of them together. The Hope Diamond has been evaluated by Lloyd's of London for it was sold several times, but now it doesn't matter what the value of these two diamonds is, for they will never be sold again. They are priceless. They are our own; they belong to America. They are ours forever."

I went back to my hotel room thinking of his words, "They are ours forever." I opened my Bible at the third chapter of Malachi. The last few verses took on new meaning to me. You remember one sentence reads, "*They shall be mine*, saith the Lord of hosts, in that day when I make up *my jewels*" (v. 17). I wondered why God would use such beautifully extravagant praise. I wondered who could be so precious to God that he would call them "my jewels." I turned to the first of Malachi's book and read it through. Then I understood.

Malachi prophesied in the midnight of the religious life of Israel. In the captions above the chapters, some editions of the Bible use these words: "indicted," "reproach," "ordeal," "neglect." Each of the four chapters rebukes the people for their sins. Even when Malachi tells them of the coming of the Messiah, he asks, "But who may abide the day of his coming? and who shall stand when he appeareth? for he is like a refiner's fire, and like fullers' sope: And he shall sit as a refiner and purifier of silver: and he shall purify the sons of Levi, and purge them as gold and silver" (Mal. 3:2-3).

Through Malachi God poured out his wrath upon his Chosen People because of their disloyalty and corruption. The whole book is like a violent thunderstorn that suddenly ceases for a little while. At the sixteenth verse of the third chapter his voice seems to grow quiet and gentle and you find these words: "Then they that feared the Lord spake often one to another: and the Lord hearkened, and heard it, and a book of remembrance was written before him for them that feared the Lord, and that thought upon his name. And they shall be mine, saith the Lord of hosts, in that day when I make up my jewels; and I will spare them, as a man spareth his own son that serveth him" (vv. 16-17).

These two verses are like a brilliant cluster of beautiful diamonds set in pig iron. I think God called this little group "my jewels" because they were faithful and good, though surrounded by a godless environment. The pressure on them must have been terrific, and the sneers and the jibes and ridicule were almost unbearable. I am sure the wild, godless crowd around them made life miserable for them. They probably suffered physically as well as mentally. Despite it all, this little group remained faithful, and God, looking down from above, hugged them to his heart and called them a beautiful name—used nowhere else in his book—"my jewels."

I

God's jewels, like the rare stones we value so highly, are *often found in unexpected places*. Surely this was true in the time that Malachi lived. It is still true, even as God's Word says, "some have entertained angels unawares" (Heb. 13:2).

The most popular lecture ever delivered in this country of ours was called "Acres of Diamonds." It was written by Russell Conwell. His introductory story was about a pagan priest who owned a compound in South Africa. Through the compound ran a little creek. The priest often became impatient when his camel took so long to nuzzle away the glittering stones in the shallow water to make a hole deep enough for him to drink comfortably. The priest thought nothing of the stones, even when the "diamond fever" spread over South Africa. Caught up in the excitement, he sold the compound and went with the others in search of diamonds. Years later, frustrated and unsuccessful, he returned to find that the biggest diamond mine of the country was on his old compound.

In the four times I listened to that lecture, Dr. Conwell applied the thought to two different things: First, we are surrounded by opportunities as precious as diamonds, if we had eyes to see them; second, we are surrounded by people who have the potentials to be diamonds in God's kingdom and in the affairs of the world. What a pity we do not have eyes that can see and ears that can hear.

Look a moment at the New Testament. Who of his contemporaries would have picked Matthew Levi as the man God would use to write an immortal Gospel story of Jesus? He was a hated, despised tax collector. Who would have selected Mark, the deserter, to give us the best picture of the strong Son of God? Who would have selected the unknown physician Luke to give to the world the tender picture of the compassionate Christ? Who would have selected three unlettered fishermen to be the "pillars" of the first church? Who would have selected Paul, a murderer and a Pharisee, to be named the ambassador to the Gentiles? With reverence, we might ask, who would have suspected that a man from Nazareth was the promised Messiah. The Wise Men looked to find the king in Herod's palace, not in a stable.

One day a Presbyterian missionary to Cuba found a little boy who had been born with only half a face. He had no mouth, and no nose; just a gaping unsightly hole. The sight of him finally became unbearable to the missionary. He implored the Board of World Missions to bring the boy to America to see if plastic surgery could at least cover up the horrible hole. After a number of operations the last bandage was taken off. The boy looked in the mirror and wept with joy. He went outside the hospital and down on his knees he kissed the ground with his new lips. The Board of World Missions kept him here and gave him an education. His gratitude was so deep he studied hard. His mind was unusually quick and he stayed in college long enough to earn a Ph.D. degree. Then back to Cuba he went to become President Rodrigues of the Presbyterian school in Havana. God's jewels do come from unexpected places.

II

Prized jewels are not man-made—they are *God-created*. Man has tried and partially succeeded in making synthetic

diamonds and rubies. He has found how to bring into exist-
ence oyster pearls—by placing grains of sand in the shell of a
live oyster—but he has never been able to *create* a *real pearl.*
He has discovered that many precious stones are the result of
pressure and heat. Likewise, we have discovered that God
often used affliction, trouble, and disappointments to shape
and polish those whom he called "my jewels."

Read again the story of the boy, pampered and spoiled by a
rich father, who was suddenly seized by his wild, half-
brothers and lowered into a cistern long enough for them to
decide *how* to put him to death. Then he was sold into
slavery, only to be falsely condemned and sent to a vermin-
filled prison. Why all of these calamities? Could Joseph's
words to his brethren, years later, be the right answer, "Now
therefore be not grieved, nor angry with yourselves, that ye
sold me hither: for God did send me before you to preserve
life. . . . So now it was not you that sent me hither, but God:
and he hath made me a father to Pharaoh, and lord of all his
house, and a ruler throughout all the land of Egypt" (Gen.
45:5–8). Whatever interpretation we put on these words of
Joseph, he thought, yes firmly believed, God's design was for
him to suffer and endure the hardships that he might be shaped
and fitted to fill this place of great responsibility. He was not
blaming his brethren nor was he blaming God.

God used a different method in preparing Abraham to be
one of his jewels. First, he answered the earnest prayers of
Abraham and gave him the promised son, Isaac. Then one day
when the boy had entwined his fingers in the heartstrings of
Abraham, God gave the old patriarch a terrible command,
"Take Isaac, thy son, up to Mount Moriah and offer him as a
sacrifice. Carry with you wood for an altar and a knife with
which to slay him."

It's hard to keep back the tears as we read that story today.

It was a long journey and one in which Abraham must have died a dozen deaths. There was nothing in the world that he loved quite as much as he loved Isaac, and though he didn't understand the "why" of God's command, he made the journey. It didn't help at all for his trusting son to keep asking, "Where is the sacrifice?" Abraham didn't have the heart to answer that question. When they arrived on the mountain, he even built the altar and took out the knife with which to kill the dearest thing on earth to him. It was then that God stayed his arm and told him the sacrifice was not to be Isaac but the ram that was caught in the bushes nearby.

We need not look in the Old Testament nor the New to find this truth. The life of one of the past presidents of Mary Hardin-Baylor College beautifully illustrates it. While on the Board of Trustees, I heard him tell the story of his conversion:

"I lived in the mountains and attended Sunday school at a little one-room church. We had a revival and I was the only one converted. After the last service a group of men were unhitching their horses to go home, when one of them said, in a disgusted tone of voice, 'This revival was a plumb failure. Only one little boy was converted.' I was dumbfounded, for I thought it was the greatest revival in the world.

"For many days I was miserable, and then I made up my mind that I would show them that it wasn't a failure. When I graduated from high school with high honors, I thought maybe this would change their minds, but no word of encouragement was spoken by any of them. Then I graduated from college with the highest marks in the class and I thought to myself, 'They are going to have to take that back now. That revival wasn't a failure.' To make a long story short, that sentence was a continual spur and it drove me throughout my life, even after I became president of Mary Hardin-Baylor.

"One day the thought came to me that maybe God had something to do with those words that were spoken that night in the dark, outside of the little one-room church. Maybe he used them to make me exert myself to the limit of my strength. Maybe I would never have been elected to the presidency of this great college if those words had not been spoken."

III

Out of what are God's jewels made? While most of us do not know the ingredients of a diamond or a ruby, we do know, because the Bible tells us, the ingredients of "God's jewels."

Humility.—Alas, many who think they are worthy may never find their names in "The Book of Remembrance," that Malachi mentions, nor be called "my jewels" by our Heavenly Father.

You remember the story of the Pharisee and the publican who went up to the Temple to pray. "The Pharisee stood and *prayed thus with himself*, God, I thank thee, that I am not as other men are, extortioners, unjust, adulterers, or even as this publican. I fast twice in the week, I give tithes of all that I possess" (Luke 18:11–12). Then followed the prayer of the publican and the Master's evaluation of both. "The publican, standing afar off, would not lift up so much as his eyes unto heaven, but smote upon his breast, saying, God be merciful to me a sinner. I tell you, this man went down to his house justified rather than the other: for every one that exalteth himself shall be abased; and he that humbleth himself shall be exalted" (vv. 13–14).

Just as men have been dumbfounded to find beautiful pearls in the mouth of the muddy Mississippi River, so Jesus tells us that many people will be surprised in the judgment day. "The

King shall answer and say unto them, Verily I say unto you, Inasmuch as ye have done it unto one of the least of these my brethren, ye have done it unto me" (Matt. 25:40).

Dedication—Most of us who go regularly to church hear the preacher use the words "surrender" and "dedicate" so often that they slip off our minds without making much impression. Let me try to make them live with this incident.

Carl Steele, head of the Art School at Wheaton College, and I were in a revival in Georgia. Many people came to church an hour early to get a good seat where they could see the picture that Carl drew. Every picture was a mighty sermon. At breakfast one morning I asked Carl how he got started drawing sermons. He waited a little before answering.

"It isn't a short story so I'll just give you the gist of it. God made it plain to me that he wanted me to preach. The only thing I wanted to do was paint pictures. I had wanted to be an artist even when I was a boy. I kept on painting and God kept on talking to me. Finally, with a heavy heart, I *surrendered*. I told God he could have the brushes, and the canvas, the tubes of paint, and I would do whatever he wanted me to do."

Carl paused for a long time, then continued: "Hardly a week passed before I found myself painting on canvas the "word pictures" God had put in his Bible. Some of them thrilled me so that I went to my pastor and fearfully asked if I could draw one at the evening service."

Here Carl stopped. I urged him to talk on. With a faraway look, he said, "I guess that's all except that I realized joyously that God did not want me to give up my brushes—he wanted me to use them and all my talents. But remember this, God didn't tell me that until I had *dedicated* my life to him."

Yes, dedication, surrender, and humility will all be present when the "Great Craftsman" makes up his jewels.

8
Scarlet Sins

W. R. Alexander, who for many years was executive secretary of the Relief and Annuity Board of the Southern Baptist Convention, for a while was pastor in a city of about twelve thousand people. Out on the edge of the city, there lived a terrible old character, known to all of us only as Old Miss Sadie. She was despised and held in contempt by everybody who knew her. When people wanted to say something was ugly or mean, they would say it was as ugly or as mean as Old Miss Sadie. If they wanted to say something was lowdown and despicable, it was as bad as Old Miss Sadie. To tell anyone he or she was as bad as Old Miss Sadie was the crowning insult. Dr. Alexander tells the story:

"We engaged Gipsy Smith, Jr. to come and hold a tent revival. The Protestant churches of the city co-operated. The Spirit of God got hold of all of us. The revival spread to the very limits of the city—even out to where Old Miss Sadie lived. Two ladies, with a lot of compassion in their hearts, went out and visited her and invited her to the meeting. She just laughed at them, and said, 'You wouldn't have me in your church if I did come, and if God did save me.' They left in confusion, but went back again and begged Old Miss Sadie to come. She laughed at them again, but they went back the third time.

"She finally consented to go if they would let her sit in a chair in the dark beyond the light of the tent. Five nights she sat out there. The two ladies, bless their hearts, sat out there with her. The sixth night she came in and sat on the back seat. Through something the preacher said, God came straight into her heart and Old Miss Sadie said out loud, 'Praise the Lord.' Everybody around her turned to look. When the invitation was given, she walked to the front.

"There was a great stir through the whole congregation. Many were dismayed and afraid that she might want to join their church. Nobody wanted Old Miss Sadie. Baptists, Methodists, Presbyterians, all of them were afraid. They just hoped she wouldn't come to their church.

"Sunday morning came after the revival service, and I was in the pulpit when Old Miss Sadie walked in the door and sat down on the back seat. You could see the whole congregation move a little, just like the wind blowing across a wheat field. Everybody fidgeted. I gave the invitation, and she stepped out into the aisle and started to the front. A wave of resentment swept over the congregation.

"Then I saw the most beautiful thing I ever saw in church. In the choir back of me was a girl of about nineteen, the antithesis of Miss Sadie—pure as the driven snow, lovely, sweet, innocent, adorable, she was just everybody's sweetheart. She was such a beautiful character. She seemed to sense the situation, pushed the choir door open, and walked right down over the pulpit and met Miss Sadie four seats from the front. She took that old, haggard face in her hands and kissed Miss Sadie's forehead. She slipped her arm through Miss Sadie's and sat down with her on the front seat.

"Suddenly, the resentment changed to shame. Some of the people even wept. We received Old Miss Sadie into our church and she never missed a service until we buried her. And one of the biggest funerals I ever had was the funeral of Miss Sadie. Maybe one of the greatest sermons on the power of God to change a life was the conversion of Miss Sadie."

There are three principal messages in this book of Isaiah. God told Isaiah to preach about *punishment* and what sin does to people; *repentance* and what people need to do; *mercy* and *forgiveness* which God offers to the whole world. Isaiah was so dedicated that he did a strange thing (nowhere else in the Bible will you find it). He had two boys. He named one of them a long, Hebrew name that means "punishment." Translated literally, it means "descending upon the prey—to kill, to punish." The other boy he named a long, Hebrew name that means "mercy—a remnant shall be spared." Isaiah didn't have any more children, so he wore sackcloth and ashes next to his skin to symbolize "repentance."

Look at these three things for they concern every one of us.

I

Punishment.—Punishment for sin may come in the most unexpected or strange way, but it always comes. A price tag is attached to every evil thing we do. God punishes us; others punish us; our own consciences punish us. "The wicked flee when no man pursueth" (Prov. 28:1).

All of us know this without even reading it in our Bibles. Isaiah stands alone in expressing this truth in such a variety of ways. We read in chapter 1, "But if ye refuse and rebel, ye shall be devoured with the sword: for the mouth of the Lord hath spoken it" (v. 20). In the second chapter, verses 17 through 19, he enlarges the picture. "The loftiness of man shall be bowed down, and the haughtiness of men shall be made low: and the Lord alone shall be exalted in that day. . . . The idols he shall utterly abolish. . . . They shall go into the holes of the rocks, and into the caves of the earth, for fear of the Lord, and for the glory of his majesty, when he ariseth to shake terribly the earth."

Still another metaphor is used in chapter 3; "Moreover the Lord saith, Because the daughters of Zion are haughty, and walk with stretched forth necks and wanton eyes, walking and mincing as they go, and making a tinkling with their feet: Therefore the Lord will smite with a scab the crown of the head of the daughters of Zion, and the Lord will discover their secret parts. In that day the Lord will take away the bravery of their tinkling ornaments about their feet, and their cauls, and their round tires like the moon, the chains, and the bracelets, and the mufflers" (vv. 16–19).

We know without being told that God punishes sin. A dramatic example is the story in the book of Esther about Haman and Mordecai. Haman, who was next to the king in power, enjoyed his prestige, for the king had ordered everyone in the empire to bow down when Haman passed. He became furious one day because a Jew by the name of Mordecai refused this kind of a salute. Mordecai's religion forbade him to bow or kneel to any human being. This kind of a salute was only for God. You will recall that Shadrach, Meshach, and Abednego likewise refused to bow to the image of the emperor. Haman felt he was too great a man for his pride to be satisfied with the elimination of one little man—Mordecai.

Knowing that Mordecai was a Jew, Haman planned to destroy all of Mordecai's race. When his plan had been approved by the thoughtless emperor and sealed with the emperor's ring, he decided to enhance his own joy, his own satisfaction, by building a scaffold fifty cubits high in the patio of his own home and hanging Mordecai on it. As you know, a cubit is the distance between your elbow and the tip of your fingers, roughly a foot and a half, so that scaffold was about seventy-five feet high. This is a fair measure of the furious revenge that Haman planned. However, God blocked his scheme. "So they hanged Haman on the gallows that he had prepared for Mordecai. Then was the king's wrath pacified" (Esther 7:10).

"Whatsoever a man soweth, that shall he also reap." Not only does God punish us *for the things we do,* he punishes us for the evil we plan to do. The "intent" not only finds a big place in our human courts of law, it finds a bigger place in God's courts. Jesus' own words emphasize this, "As a man thinketh in his heart, so is he."

A Virginia newspaper carried a story of a thing that happened in Kentucky some years ago. A man by the name of Lucien served the state of Kentucky "beyond the call of duty." In deep appreciation, twice he was honored in the legislature. Then one day he discovered that an old friend whose first name was Sam was in the penitentiary and had eight more years to serve. Lucien was badly shaken. He went to the warden and asked if he might talk to Sam. The warden was delighted and honored that Lucien should come. He said, "I'll bring Sam to my office and you may talk to him as long as you like." They talked for nearly two hours. Finally they were both laughing at some incidents in their youth, for they had been reared together. Lucien went back home and Sam went back to his cell.

A month later Lucien paid a visit to the Governor. "I haven't been able to sleep. Sam, my boyhood buddy, is in prison. He was a good boy, Governor, and since you told me once that if there was anything Kentucky could do for me to name it, I came here to ask if there is any way in the world for you to give him a pardon. If there is, I'll take him into my business and into my home, for he has no family, and I have a big house."

The Governor answered: "Let me talk to the Board of Parole and some others."

A week later he sent for Lucien and said: "Here's the pardon, but it's yours under one condition; that is, that you sit down in the warden's office and talk with Sam for two more hours. Then if you think you should give him the pardon, take Sam home. I will parole him to you."

Lucien smiled, "I'll be back up here in two hours with Sam." He hurried over to the penitentiary and again they sat down in the warden's office. This time Lucien said, "Sam, when you get out of here, will you go into business with me? I might even get you out of here sooner than you expect."

Sam got up and walked around awhile, looked out of the window, then said, "I don't believe I could accept that invitation, for I've got something to do when I get out of here, something very important. I'm going to do it just as soon as I get out of here."

"What is it, Sam?" Lucien asked.

Sam turned around and fire glinted from his eyes, hatred filled his whole face as he said, "When I get out of here, I am going to get two men together—the judge who sent me up here and one witness—and I'm going to kill them both with my bare hands."

Lucien left the warden's office, Sam went back to his cell. Lucien stood outside the gates of the prison and tore up that pardon. God punishes us for our evil desires, daydreams, and resentments.

Beloved, something ugly, something mean, something vicious, something terrible can fill our lives so that we would not accept the most beautiful invitation that ever came to the ears and the hearts of men—God's invitation. "Come now, let us reason together, saith the Lord: though your sins be as scarlet, they shall be as white as snow; though they be red like crimson, they shall be as wool" (Isa. 1:18).

II

Repentance.—I am sure that too often we preachers have omitted a most important fact in preaching on the necessity of repentance. I know I'm guilty. How many times we have used our *sternest,* even *harshest,* voice as we called on people to repent. We have warned them that if they do not repent they will be lost. Of course, this is true. But the thing we neglect to say is written three times in the fifteenth chapter of Luke. Jesus ended the parable of the lost sheep with this sentence: "When he cometh home, he calleth together his friends and neighbours, saying unto them, *Rejoice with me;* for I have found my sheep which was lost. *I say unto you, that likewise joy shall be in heaven over one sinner that repenteth, more than over ninety and nine just persons, which need no repentance*" (vv. 6–7). Then he closed the parable of the lost coin like this: "When she hath found it, she calleth her friends and her neighbours together, saying, *Rejoice with me;* for I have found the piece which I had lost. Likewise, *I say unto you, there is joy in the presence of the angels of God over one sinner that repenteth*" (vv. 9–10).

The story of the prodigal son has written all over it the joy of the father because of the repentance and return of his son. "But the father said to his servants, Bring forth the best robe, and put it on him; and put a ring on his hand, and shoes on his feet: and bring hither the fatted calf, and kill it; and let us eat, and be merry: for this my son was dead, and is alive again; he was lost, and is found. And they began to be merry" (Luke 15:22–24). Listen to the closing statement: "It was meet that we should make merry, and be glad: for this thy brother was dead, and is alive again; and was lost, and is found" (v. 32).

The beautiful truth about repentance, which we so often do not mention, is the happiness and the joy in heaven that repentance brings. Warren Huyck, of Lumberton, North Carolina, recently sent me a perfect illustration of this truth.

The story of an English home in World War I concerns a widowed mother whose only son had died on the fields of Flanders. Her bitterness was the more acute because her neighbor with five sons had been spared any loss, while she had lost both husband and son. Continuously mourning the death of her boy, she refused to be reconciled. One night she dreamed that an angel appeared and said to her, "You may have your dear one again for ten minutes. At what period of his life do you wish him to return to you? As a cooing babe upon your breast, as a little chubby-fisted, starry-eyed toddler about your feet, or as a little lad starting school, a youth just completing his course in school, or the young soldier in his brave new uniform with the shining brass buttons, journeying away to the battlefield?"

The mother meditated a bit, then replied: "I want him back, but on none of these occasions. I think I would like best his return when once I denied his request and remained firm in spite of his insistence. He, in a fit of anger, cried out, 'I hate you—I don't like you any more, and I won't stay with you,' then rushed away into the garden. When his anger had abated, he came back to me, his grimy, wistful face stained with tears, and, holding out his little arms, with quivering lip he said: 'Muvver, I'm so sorry I was a naughty boy. I won't be bad any more ever. I *love* you and want you to hug me again.' Give him back to me and let me feel him clinging close to me while he sobs his little heart out in sorrow and love. That's when I loved him best."

Thus does the repentant sense the unfailing love of the Father and his unending mercy. Many people are convinced they are sinners—their own consciences convict them—but this isn't repentance. It isn't enough to realize you have done wrong and need forgiveness. It isn't enough for you to believe that Jesus is God's Son and the Saviour of the world and do nothing about it.

Years ago when I was in Richmond College, just beginning to preach, this great truth was made plain to me by a grand old minister. He was my uncle, and his name was Baker Boatwright. He was the father of the president of Richmond College. It was at his invitation that I went up from Richmond College to spend a weekend and preach for him at old Mt. Zion Baptist Church. I had prepared a sermon on "Repentance," selecting for the text those words in the fifteenth chapter of Luke where it is said of the prodigal son, he "came to himself." The whole sermon was woven around the importance of a man's "coming to himself" and being convicted of his sin and his need of forgiveness.

After church Uncle Baker and I got into his buggy to return to his home. We drove in silence for a couple of miles. When I couldn't stand it any longer, I said, "Uncle Baker, was the sermon so bad that you just don't want to talk about it?"

He answered, "Roy, you were exactly right in saying, 'It was a great day when he came to himself.' But you implied that that was repentance. That was a bad mistake. You could preach to a hundred sinners and maybe every one of them would say, 'I am sorry for the things I have done that were wrong.' He could sit there and weep. *That's conviction.* But that isn't enough. No one was ever saved just by being convicted of his sin. He has to *do* something about it. He has to do what Jesus said that prodigal did. He got up and went back to his father and tried to tell him, 'I have sinned against heaven, and in thy sight, and am no longer worthy to be called thy son.' His father never let him finish, but said, even as our Heavenly Father will say, 'This is my son who was dead, and is alive again. Come, let us make merry and rejoice."

III

Mercy.—"Come now, and let us reason together, saith the Lord: though your sins be as scarlet, they shall be as white as snow; though they be red like crimson, they shall be as wool" (Isa. 1:18). I don't suppose anyone ever read this verse without wondering what Isaiah had in mind when he used the two words "scarlet" and "crimson" to describe the sins that God's mercy would wipe out. Maybe we would all agree that Isaiah was talking about the worst and most despicable sins. The solemn thought comes to me that the sins that weigh the heaviest on the scales of man may not be the weightiest on God's scales.

When we read the story of Jesus in every one of the Gospels, we find him scorching the people who were committing what, alas, we often call "respectable" sins. We all know he called the Pharisees "whited sepulchers" because they paraded their piety before men. Their inconsistency seemed to irritate Christ more than almost anything that happened to him on earth. Their pride, their envy, their jealousy hurt him deeply. These were the sins that crucified Christ. Surely they belong among the scarlet and crimson sins.

Not long ago I preached in a church in which I had held three revivals in the last ten years. After the first morning service, the pastor and I went out to lunch, and he asked me to please make one visit while I was in the city. So, the next morning I called the owner of a big cotton factory and said to him, "Do you have time to talk to an old friend for a few minutes?" Eagerly he answered, "Please come right down to my office."

As I went into his office, I said, "I came to sympathize with you in the terrible trouble that has come to you. You have always been such a fine Christian and so consistently lived the kind of life that Jesus wants us all to live, it just seems, to an army of your friends, that it doesn't make sense for you to have to suffer."

He got up from his desk and walked around the room for a while and then said, "Roy, I hang my head in shame every time I think of what this younger brother of mine has done. In a moment of anger and wrath he hit a man so hard that when he fell and struck his head on the pavement he died." He was silent for a while and then continued, "Sometimes I get angry, even with you and the other ministers. You spend so much time preaching against liquor and gambling but so little time preaching against the wreckers of life like anger, envy, and jealousy. *These* are the things that put my brother behind prison bars. Every one of them is worse than whiskey and gambling."

I sat there for a long time and thought about these "scarlet sins" and how those very sins crucified my Saviour. There are other scarlet sins, just as dangerous that belong in the same category. Think how many homes have been wrecked by sins of disposition. Jesus pictured one of them when he told of that elder brother who didn't go in to the feast. He also told the parable of ten virgins, five of whom had acquired the habit of procrastination and carelessness which cost them their lives. When they arrived at the wedding, the doors were shut. Jesus actually was saying it cost them their souls. Any sin that can cost one his soul is surely a "scarlet" sin.

I think it is about these words that God had Isaiah write the text, "Come now, and let us reason together, saith the Lord:

though your sins be as scarlet, they shall be as white as snow; though they be red like crimson, they shall be as wool." This is a glorious promise. It is so beautiful that it has been set to music and sung across the world. Look at the words:

> Though your sins be as scarlet,
> They shall be as white as snow;
> Though they be red like crimson,
> They shall be as wool.
> He'll forgive your transgressions,
> And remember them no more.

A fellow pastor told me of the funeral of an old country doctor. He said that a half-dozen men spoke at the service. Each one, overflowing with deep emotion, related some of the grand things in the old doctor's life. Among them they mentioned that he always went, night or day, wherever he was needed; and, since he never sent out bills, probably half of the county owed him money. He was a bachelor and often said to poor people, "Don't worry about paying me. I don't have much expense, anyhow."

When it came time for the preacher to speak, he began, "Let me be fanciful. When our beloved doctor died, God sent Gabriel after him to take him to heaven. On the way the doctor aroused enough to ask, 'Where are you taking me?'

"Gabriel answered, 'In my Father's house are many mansions. One is waiting for you.' After a long silence, the old doctor spoke again, 'What about my sins?'

"Gabriel smiled and said, 'God buried them.'

"Again a long time elapsed before the doctor asked, 'Gabriel, where did God bury them?'

"Gabriel answered quietly, 'He has forgotten.'"

The words of the song are true. "He will forgive our transgressions and remember them no more."

9

What Doest Thou Here?

When as a boy I first read this story recorded in the nineteenth chapter of 1 Kings, it was such a disturbing story I turned back and read it again. This time I underscored two sentences that God spoke to Elijah. The first was a question and implied an accusation: *"What doest thou here?"* (v. 9). I have an idea that question scorched the old prophet's heart. The second was a command and implied a disappointed God: "Go, return on thy way . . . and Elisha the son of Shaphat of Abelmeholah shalt thou *anoint to be prophet in thy room"* (vv. 15–16).

In the margin of my Bible, I wrote, "He failed his final examinations." I'm glad God didn't dismiss him then and there. The record shows God forgave him and sent him on another mission. Also he gave him the responsibility of training Elisha for the tasks ahead. Then God sent a chariot to take him home.

Look for a moment at the setting of this question, "What doest thou here?" and the reason God asked it. Elijah had had a thrilling, glorious mountaintop experience. He had challenged King Ahab to bring all of the prophets of Baal up on

Mount Carmel. They were to build an altar and place on it a sacrifice to their gods. Likewise, he would build an altar and put a burnt offering on it to his God. He would give the prophets of Baal all day to call on their gods to accept their offerings and consume them with fire. All Elijah asked for was a few minutes late in the evening. Whichever god answered by fire would be the god that King Ahab and all the nation would worship. So, all day long the Baalites called on their gods. The gods never answered. Elijah chided them, "Call louder, they may be asleep."

In the evening Elijah had barrels of water poured over his altar and then lifted his arms up to heaven. He prayed to the Lord to accept the offering. Suddenly the fire flashed so hot that even the stones of the altar were consumed. The ditches that ran full of water were licked dry. Elijah took a sword and put to death the prophets of Baal, and the God of Israel was crowned. A little later Elijah turned to Ahab: "The famine is over; the rain is coming. But the dust is ankle deep between here and Samaria. You had better start with your chariots or you won't get there, because the dust is going to be mud in a few minutes. The rain will be coming down in torrents. Then Elijah girded his loins, jerked his sash tight, and ran in front of that chariot. He was exuberant. God had given him a great victory. But he had been in Samaria only a few minutes when Jezebel, Ahab's queen, sent him a message, "I will do to you, before this time tomorrow, what you did to the prophets of Baal."

The next time we see Elijah, he is out in the wilderness under a juniper tree, feeling sorry for himself, even rebellious. God left him alone for a while. Weary from the long flight, he slept until an angel of the Lord awakened him and commanded him to eat. There before him he saw a cruse of water and a barley cake. He ate and went back to sleep. Again, an angel aroused him and told him to eat and drink and go to Horeb, the mountain of God, for God had something to say to him.

Forty days later, while Elijah sat in a cave at Horeb, the voice of God asked, "What doest thou here, Elijah?"

The old prophet's answer did not please God, for it implied that God had not been powerful enough to protect his own prophet. He said to God, "I have been very jealous for the Lord God of hosts: for the children of Israel have forsaken thy covenant, thrown down thine altars, and slain thy prophets with the sword; and I, even I only, am left; and they seek my life, to take it away" (v. 10).

God said, "Elijah, step to the mouth of the cave. I have something to show you." Elijah walked out, and God dramatized his power. The wind blew so hard it tore off part of the mountain, then came an earthquake and everything trembled, and rocks tumbled around him; a roaring fire swept by. In the stillness that followed, God asked the same question the second time, "What doest thou here, Elijah?" (v. 13).

Elijah gave him the same whining answer.

Then God said to Elijah, "Go back to the wilderness, go by Samaria, anoint Hazael, go down through Israel, anoint Jehu, king of Israel, then find Elisha and take the mantle off your shoulders and put it on his, for he shall be my prophet in your room." I imagine the journey God sent him on was dismal and heartbreaking. Certainly the part that took him to Elisha's home was a trying experience. When he saw the man who was to take his place, he whipped off his mantle, threw it over the shoulders of Elisha, and fled.

I

Now, look closely at God's question. On which of these words did God put the emphasis? Wherever he placed it, it carried a stern rebuke. It is a searching question that each of us might well ask ourselves ever and anon. Did God ask it like this? "What doest *thou* here, Elijah? Of all the people in the world, Elijah, What doest *thou* here? It hasn't been very long since I sent ravens to feed you, when I had you tucked away and hidden in another wilderness. Nor has it been very long since I told you to go out and face Ahab. You weren't even a little afraid. You walked down that dusty road and met one of Ahab's right-hand lieutenants, and you said to him, 'Go tell Ahab I want to talk to him.' And the man answered in consternation, 'I've always been your friend, Elijah, don't you know that Ahab has put a tremendous price on your head? He has sent couriers into every nation around us and told them "dead or alive" he will pay a huge bounty for you? You can't do this, Elijah, go and hide.'

"You just laughed at him and said, 'Go tell Ahab I want to talk to him.'

"He demurred, 'If I go tell him and he gets out here, he won't find you. You know you won't stay here and meet him.'

" 'Go tell Ahab, I'll be walking down this road.'

"When Ahab came with fifty picked men, you looked him in the eye. When he said, 'Art thou he that troubleth Israel?' you answered, 'I haven't troubled Israel. You and your wickedness and your sin have troubled Israel.'

"Then you dictated the terms and he quailed in front of you. What doest *thou* here? Of all people, with such great experiences behind you, who have been so fearless, *thou* Elijah, What doest *thou* here?"

II

Now, put the emphasis on the word *here*, and ask the question like this: "What doest thou *here?*" Was the emphasis on the word *here*—under a juniper tree? "What doest thou *here?*" I realize the distinction is very fine between these two words "thou" and "here." Have *you* ever been in some place where you knew God did not want you? Have *you* ever looked around, hoping you would not see anybody you knew? Have you slid down in your seat when you did see somebody?

"What doest thou *here*, Elijah?" I am sure the old iron man Elijah felt deep humiliation when God asked that question. He knew he had no business running away and hiding in the wilderness. However, many of us cannot condemn him because we, too, have had our consciences scorch us for going to places where Christ would not go with us.

Recently I was helping a pastor in a revival in one of the biggest churches in our Southern Baptist Convention. On Tuesday morning he came to my room at the hotel, very depressed. He said, "Last night after the service the teacher of one of my largest young men's classes asked me to stay and talk awhile with him. He was as nearly brokenhearted as any man I ever saw. He sat by my desk and sobbed a little while and then blurted out, 'Doctor, I have to resign my Sunday school class. I made one mistake and it has ruined my usefulness as a teacher.

" 'I was sent to New York to a buyers' convention. We buyers were cooped up for two days from morning until late evening. After we finished the last day, one of my friends from another city said, "Let's get a cup of coffee and a piece of pie." We relaxed for a little while and then he suggested that we go to a show down the street. When we stopped in front of it, I realized that it was a burlesque show. I hesitated for a minute and started to tell him I had never been to a burlesque show, and that I didn't feel it was any place for me to go.

" 'But, I didn't. He bought the tickets and we went in. We'd been in there about a half an hour when someone behind me reached over and touched me on the shoulder. When I turned, an accusing voice said: "Fancy meeting you here! I certainly didn't expect to see you in a burlesque." He was a member of my Sunday school class.' The teacher wept silently for a little while and then said, 'I believe I would give my right arm to live that evening over.' " But we all know there is no road back.

Jim Middleton, one of God's great preachers, told me that once when he was assisting in a Red Cross drive in his hometown, he had an upsetting experience. Among the names given to him and his partner to solicit was that of a man who owned a chain of saloons. He had made large contributions in previous years, so they went to his downtown office. His secretary said he was in another office in one of his saloons. "My partner and I were stumped," he said. "Neither of us wanted to go into a saloon, but we very much needed his pledge for our noonday report luncheon. We went out on the sidewalk and talked it over for a while. Then we decided we would go and find him.

"When we got inside the saloon and our eyes adjusted to the semidarkness of the place, I saw the son of one of our finest Christian homes sitting at the bar, a glass of beer in front of him. To say I was shocked is an understatement. I walked over, and laid my hand on his shoulder. He turned crimson when he looked up at me. I'm sure there was accusation in my voice as I asked, '*What are you doing here?*' Before he could ask me the same question, I explained my mission. Then I told him that I was deeply grieved to find him in a place like this. After a moment he said to me, 'Dr. Middleton, please, please, please don't tell my father. I promise you I will never come in here again.' " Dr. Middleton's question was the very same question God asked Elijah when he found him in a place where he should never have been. I'm sure there was accusation in God's voice, too.

I am sure, too, that God was very stern and unhappy when he took that memorable walk in the Garden of Eden. He had come to see Adam and Eve, but they were hiding because of their disobedience. Both rebuke and disappointment were in his voice when he called unto Adam, "Where art thou?" God could well have asked the same question that he asked Elijah, "What doest thou *here*, hiding amongst the trees in the Garden?"

Jesus just looked at Simon Peter, standing by the fire, surrounded by the wrong crowd. He did not have to ask, "What doest thou *here?*"

III

Put the emphasis on the word *doest*. "What *doest* thou here, Elijah?" Just what are you doing? If Elijah had answered, and told the truth, he would have had to say, "I'm not doing anything, just sitting here under a juniper tree feeling sorry for myself. I'm just not doing *anything*." Many people lose the joy of the Christian life by not doing anything. Christianity is action. The kingdom of God is a great movement. There is nothing static about it; it is positive; it is going somewhere. There is a great message in the song we sing so lustily, "Onward, Christian soldiers, marching as to war." God has something for us to *do*.

Sometime ago I read of an incident that occurred when a theater burned and some forty people lost their lives. Sitting down close to the front of the theater were a boy and a girl. They were engaged to be married. She was wearing a large diamond ring on the third finger of her left hand. Suddenly a scream came from backstage, "Fire!" Then the smoke billowed out and there immediately followed a stampede. The boy was one of the first out of the theater. By and by, he found his girl in the crowd outside. A little embarrassed he said, "I hope you didn't get hurt." She just stood and looked at him and didn't say a word. He slipped his arm through hers as they started through the crowd, but she pulled away from him. As they walked down the street, he kept trying to talk to her, but she was silent. They came to her gate and stopped. She turned very slowly and deliberately and looked at him. She took the ring off of that third finger and handed it to him. She did not say a word. She did not need to. She did not have to give him any reason, as she walked up the steps and into the house. What had he done? *Nothing*, nothing, not a thing.

How much more wonderful it is when you can answer that question, "What *doest* thou here?" with something that will put a smile on God's face.

Sir Wilfred Grenfell, famous surgeon, spent the last two winters of his life at the Kellogg Health Sanitarium in Miami Springs, Florida. My home was about three blocks away. Because I had admired him so much for so many years, I decided that, presumptuous as it was, I was going over and introduce myself and invite him to come to my home for lunch or dinner. When I met him I both trembled and stammered, for I realized suddenly I was in the presence of royalty—God's royalty. When I finally invited him, he did not hesitate even a moment but graciously accepted. After lunch we sat on the porch which faced the golf links. I did not know that he had ever loved the game, and I was delighted that he wanted to come back some other afternoon and sit for a while and watch the players go by. He came back many times, and I was honored and delighted just to sit near him.

One day I asked him what was the most thrilling experience of his life. He answered immediately:

"It happened at the Massachusetts General Hospital, where I gave the commencement address one year. I had told the president that I was desperately in need of eight nurses for my hospital in Labrador and asked if it would be appropriate for me to call for volunteers at the end of the program. He was very much pleased and readily gave his consent.

"So, just before the services were over, I told the group of some four hundred graduate nurses that God and I needed eight nurses to go to Labrador and work for one year. I told them there would be no salary, but that a skipper of one of the ocean liners that stopped at Labrador had graciously agreed to take them there without cost and bring them back at the end of a year. All I had to offer were clothes and room and board and work. I said to them, 'You will be giving one year of your lives to God, for Jesus said, "Inasmuch as you do it unto one of the least of these, you do it unto me." ' I told them further that I worked without salary, too.

"I asked them to think about it for a minute, and then I would ask for volunteers. A murmur went up over the whole crowd as they talked to one another, and then I raised my hand for silence. I said, 'Are there eight of you who will give one year of your life to my Master?' A moment later I choked up so I could hardly speak, for about three-fourths of that class of nurses stood."

When Dr. Grenfell finished the story, both of us reached for our handkerchiefs to dry our eyes.

God needs us to be at work for him. Can you answer the question God asked Elijah, "What *doest* thou here?" with an answer that will make God smile?

10
Three Advocates

One day I was driving to a luncheon to speak to a group of Baptist preachers. The meeting place was in a part of town that was unfamiliar to me. At one point there was a veritable labyrinth of lanes, streets, and avenues crisscrossing each other. I never got to the luncheon, for some shrubbery obstructed my view and I struck a car that had a right of way.

When I finally got home, I called a deacon, Sam Wallace, who is a good attorney and a good friend, and told him that I had a traffic violation and a summons to court.

He answered like a real friend, "Send me the ticket and I will go in your place." And I said, "That's just like you, but it isn't that simple. I had a slight accident and did a little damage to another car, so I must go to court." Quickly he answered, "I will be standing by your side. I will be your advocate."

The day of the trial came. Sam and I sat together awaiting the time for me to stand before the judge. I turned to him to say, "Sam, I'm nervous—this is the first time I ever was on trial. What do I say?"

There was sympathy and understanding in his answer, "You don't say a word. I'll answer for you." When the clerk

84

called my name and we took our places before the bar, the judge turned to my advocate and asked, "How do you plead?" He answered, *Nolo contendere.* Then he explained what happened.

Without a moment's hesitation, the judge said to me, "I find you guilty." Then a smile came over his face as he continued, "But there will be no penalty. Case dismissed."

After awhile I went back to my study and opened my Bible to the second chapter of 1 John and read this wonderful promise, "If any man sin, we have an advocate with the Father, Jesus Christ the righteous" (v. 1). Opposite the word "advocate," in the margin, was written the great word "Paraclete," with the definition below it: "One who stands by." Then there were some cross references to the fourteenth and sixteenth chapters of John. Bible lovers know the word "Comforter" in these chapters is another translation of the Greek word "Paraclete." So, God's Word tells us we have two advocates—one with the Father, when we give an account of ourselves before the final judgment bar; one to be with us, even the Holy Spirit, while we walk through life.

Our hearts are filled with gratitude to our Father in heaven for these two needed advocates. Life would be awful without them. But I do not think our Heavenly Father intended that we should sit with folded hands and say, "All is taken care of—there is nothing for us to do." I am sure you have noticed that with every blessing God gives us, he also gives us a responsibility. To Abraham he said, "I will bless thee . . . *and thou shalt be a blessing*" (Gen. 12:2). So, here God expects something of us. He doesn't give us all we will need. I think he intended that we "build" another advocate. I would not dignify it with the word "Paraclete." That would be irreverent. But we do need "something" that will stand by and help us walk the "straight and narrow road."

Look first at the two God-given advocates and then at the one we should "build."

I

We have an advocate in Jesus Christ, the righteous (1 John 2:1).—It is a great comfort to know that when we stand before God's court at the final judgment, Jesus will be "standing by us." He will be out *advocate.*

G. Campbell Morgan, one of the greatest expositors in his day, spoke each evening for a week at the University of Virginia when I was a student there. The auditorium was packed every night, even to standing room. The things that he said to us crept into the classrooms each day. The last night that he was with us, he picked up his Bible and held it up high between his hands and said, "There is one key thought that runs through this Bible from cover to cover. Think a minute. Can you name it?" There was silence for a few minutes, and then he spoke again, as if he had read our minds. "No, the key word is not love, nor is it God, nor is it sin, but the key word is *relationships.* You will not find the word itself, but you will find the thought spelled out from the beginning of Genesis to the last chapter in Revelation. The Bible continually speaks about our relationship to each other, our relationship to God, our relationship to ourselves, and our relationship to our possessions."

The New Testament is focused on our relationship to Jesus Christ and the salvation that he came to bring. Over and over God pleads with us to "make friends with Jesus." We will need him when we stand before God's eternal judgment bar. We will want him to be standing by us. If we spend eternity in one of the mansions which Jesus said were "in my Father's house," it will be because our relationship with Jesus is right. We will need him to be our "advocate with the Father" on the

day we are called to give an account of ourselves. How true
that grand old song is:

> I must needs go home by the way of the cross,
>   There's no other way but this;
> I shall ne'er get sight of the gates of light,
>   If the way of the cross I miss.

R. G. Lee, one of the greatest preachers of our day, tells a
story that beautifully illustrates this:

"There was a mountain school that had a hard time keeping
a teacher, because there was a group of big, rough boys who
took pride in running the teacher off. Finally, the school
board found a young, dedicated, Christian man who agreed to
take a try at it. The bunch of young ruffians went to school on
his first day and decided that since he was a young man they
would gang up on him and give him a good licking. They
were all in their seats in the schoolroom when he arrived. Just
as he entered the room, he heard the biggest boy, whose name
was Tom, say in a stage whisper, 'Leave him to me. I can whip
him all by myself.'

"The teacher surprised them, when, with a smile he said,
'Fellows, I don't know how to run a school. I haven't had
much experience, so I want you to make the rules we'll run
by. You tell me how you want it to be, and I'll write down on
the blackboard the rules you agree to.'

"He picked up a piece of chalk and asked, 'What is the first
rule?'

"One of them said, 'Start and stop on time.'

" 'That's a good one,' and he wrote it down. A hand went
up and as the teacher nodded to him, he said, 'Twenty-minute
recesses and an hour for lunch.'

" 'Do you all agree?' the teacher asked. A chorus of 'yes'

was the answer. In quick succession they called out the others: 'No stealing,—no cheating, no homework.'

"When they could think of no more, the teacher said, 'Those rules suit me fine, but shouldn't we put some penalties by some of them? Tell me what penalties you suggest for cheating and stealing.' They finally agreed that cheating would be punished with five strokes of the rod and stealing with ten strokes, both to be given with the offender's coat off.

"Everything went well until one day Tom's lunch was stolen. A frail little boy in hand-me-down clothes that were too big for him admitted his guilt. The school demanded that he be whipped. When the teacher called the little fellow up front, he came whimpering and begging to leave his coat on. The pupils insisted he obey the rules and take off his coat. When he did, a deathly silence settled over the room, for he had no shirt on and his emaciated body looked like skin stretched over bones. The teacher gasped and dropped the rod. He knew he could never whip that little boy. Suddenly, big Tom strode up and stood between the two. 'I'll take it for him, Teacher, for after all it was my lunch he stole.' He shrugged out of his coat. At the third blow the switch broke, and the teacher threw it in the corner and said, 'That's all, school dismissed.'

"The frail little boy laid his hand on big Tom's arm and through his tears said, 'Thank you, Tom, it would have killed me.' "

It did kill Jesus when he took our place. "He was wounded for our transgressions, he was bruised for our iniquities . . . and with his stripes we are healed" (Isa. 53:5). Not only will Jesus be our advocate in that great day at the judgment seat of God, but he is our advocate with God now and will be all through our lives.

II

We have an advocate here and now.—In the fourteenth chapter of his Gospel, John quoted a promise that Jesus made: "I will pray the Father, and he shall give you another Comforter, that he may abide with you for ever" (v. 16). And again, "But the Comforter, which is the Holy Ghost, whom the Father will send in my name, he shall teach you all things, and bring all things to your remembrance, whatsoever I have said unto you" (v. 26). So, Jesus is saying, "You will always have an advocate in the Holy Spirit to help you while you live on this earth." Webster's unabridged dictionary gives a group of beautiful synonyms for the word "advocate"—counselor, strengthener, reminder, admonisher, consultant, adviser, guide, helper, defender, and comforter.

Years ago someone wrote a most comforting sentence: "The will of God will not lead us where the grace of God cannot keep us." An unknown author put the thought into verse, and then B. B. McKinney set it to music. He called the song "Never Alone."

One night at Shocco Springs, the assembly grounds of Alabama Baptists, Dr. McKinney led the congregation in singing this grand old hymn. The expression on his face and the joy with which he sang it so impressed me that after the service was over and he and I had gone up to my room, I asked him if he knew anything about the author of those words. Quickly he answered, "One thing only. The man who wrote that poem knew what trouble was and had experienced the helping hand of the Lord and the Holy Spirit as he was led safely through whatever dark road opened in front of him. Listen to this first stanza." Then he sang:

I've seen the lightning flashing,
And heard the thunder roll,

I've felt sin's breakers dashing,
Trying to conquer my soul;
I've heard the voice of Jesus,
Telling me still to fight on,
He promised never to leave me,
Never to leave me alone.
No, never alone,
No, never alone,
He promised never to leave me,
Never to leave me alone;
No, never alone,
No, never alone,
He promised never to leave me,
Never to leave me alone.

A young man, who was reared in Ten Thousand Islands, was my guide for a day of fishing in those islands in the Florida Everglades. We came into a huge bay named Chevelier. He pointed across the bay to the entrance of a creek a mile away and said, "See that creek? That's where we're going. But there's a big oyster reef, a mud flat, and some rocks between us and the creek. So I'll have to hug the shoreline." Five minutes later he cut down the throttle and the boat slowed to a crawl. I didn't have to ask why. My face expressed surprise. With a smile he said, "There is an oyster bar right in front of us." When I asked how he knew where all of those bars were, he answered simply, "I have been this way many times before."

The thought came to me that Jesus knows where all of the rough places in life are. He has walked in the paths of the world and many times bumped into evil ideas and evil people. What a consolation to have him as a guide through the tangled paths of life. When we need help or protection we can have *a defender* walking beside us.

W. F. Powell, for many years pastor of the First Baptist

Church of Nashville, Tennessee, related this incident from his own experience:

"I was riding a mule home after hoeing corn all afternoon, when I came to a closed gate on our farm. I got off the mule to open the gate, led him through, and tied him on the other side. Just as I closed the gate, I heard a pitiful cry. I couldn't quite decide what it was, and then I saw a bird on the ground that looked for all the world like it was drunk. Its feathers were fluffed out, its wings drooped, and it staggered haltingly along. Its head rolled from side to side and I wondered what in the world was the matter with it.

"Then I saw not far away a large, black snake, looking straight at the bird, his tongue flipping in and out and his head moving ever so slowly from side to side. I did not know anything about hypnotism, but I did know what to do. I grabbed the hoe and circled around behind that black snake and *cut his tail off*. The bird dropped and lay motionless. I decided to watch it for a little while to see if it had died or would revive. A few minutes later it moved and pulled in one wing, then the other. After a little it stood tottering, looking up at a low branch of a sapling. Finally, it flew up to that low limb. A little later it moved to a branch higher up. I watched it until it sat in the top of that tree and I was hoping to hear it sing, but I decided I had wasted enough time and had better get on home. As I rode along, I thought of a verse of Scripture that had been put into song,

> He breaks the power of cancelled sin,
> He sets the Pris'ner free;
> His blood can make the foulest clean,
> His blood availed for me."

Once more I say it is wonderful to have a comforter, an advocate, a helper, a defender—here on earth, as well as hereafter.

III

The third advocate, for want of a better word, I have chosen to call a "stockpile of righteous living." I have no Scripture reference for it, except Jeremīah 13:23, Which reads, "Can the Ethiopian change his skin, or the leopard his spots? then may ye also do good, that are accustomed to do evil." Wouldn't it be almost, if not quite, true that the reverse of this thought is also true? Could it not be read like this: "Can the Ethiopian change his skin, or the leopard his spots, then could you also do evil that are accustomed to do good?"

The writer to the Ephesians tells us we should grow in grace and in the knowledge of Christ and that our aim should be to attain to "the measure of the stature of the fulness of Christ" (Eph. 4:13). In other words, when we have reached some maturity in the Christian life and are growing steadily toward the measure of the stature of Christ, we have something to lean on. Since we have established habits of doing only what will please God, it becomes easier and easier for us to walk that straight and narrow road. Likewise, it becomes harder and harder for us to think contrary to our Master's wishes. In a sense we have built up, not a *defender*, but a *defense*.

We know the Holy Spirit will rebuke us and will, as Jesus said, "remind us of all the things that he had said unto us."

Wasn't it Shakespeare who said, "Conscience doth make cowards of us all"? I would like to paraphrase it and say also, "Conscience doth make kings of us all." When we have chosen the high road and traveled it awhile, our consciences yell at us if we even look at the low road. Maybe, in this sense we *are* cowards. The Bible tells us in both the first and the fifth chapters of Revelation that we are kings. Does not this imply that because we live on such a high plane we should do no wrong? Christ put tremendous emphasis on consistency in

Christian living. The most stinging things he ever said were directed at the religious leaders of his day. Their inconsistency hurt him deeply. Inconsistency still hurts him today. It also ruins our witness.

I had to smile the other day when a pastor told of this incident. He said one of his deacons was following Arnold Palmer around the golf course in a tournament. Arnold, as you know, has won all of the big tournaments in the world and today is an outstanding champion in golfing circles. The first chance the deacon had to look at Arnold's golf ball came on the seventeenth hole, where he, the deacon, had purposefully gone out on the edge of the fairway to the place where he thought Arnold's drive would stop. Before the crowd reached there, he ran out and got down on his knees so he could see the make of the golf ball that Arnold was using. The pastor said, "I wonder what he would have thought if the ball had not carried the name of the golf balls that Arnold was advertising on television."

I wonder, too, sometimes what people think of us who profess to be followers of Christ when we fail to act or look or talk like Christians. One thing we should never forget, and that is we are Christ's representatives in this world. People who see us and know us and listen to us are going to evaluate the worth of Christianity by what they see in us. Let me illustrate:

In Charlottesville, Virginia, I was chairman of the committee to secure a speaker for the Kiwanis Club on Washington's birthday. It was to be a gala occasion to which our wives and friends had been invited. A prominent speaker from Richmond, Virginia, had accepted our invitation. About three hours before the time for the luncheon, I received a long distance call that he was ill and could not be present. Quickly I called the other two men on the committee, and we all agreed that there was just one man in Charlottesville who could replace the speaker on such short notice. The man was John Metcalfe, dean of the Graduate School of the University of Virginia.

I got in my car and drove to the University as quickly as possible. I explained my predicament to Dr. Metcalfe, and among the things I said to him was this: "You wouldn't have to prepare a formal address. Just come and talk to us about George Washington."

A frown came over his face, and very slowly he pushed back his chair from his desk and walked over in front of the window. For a while he stood there silently, then he turned and answered: "Roy, you have forgotten something. I am dean of one of the greatest universities in America. When I stand up to speak, the University of Virginia is speaking. If I were not connected with the University I would say "yes" to you in a moment, but no matter what kind of an explanation you made to the Kiwanis Club, I am still a representative of this great school. I can't afford to make a speech that isn't worthy of the position that I hold."

What a grand thing it would be if we Christian people would always remember that there are some places we must not go; some things we must not do; some words we must not use, because we are representatives of Christ and Christianity.

11
God's Cowboys

Some sixty years ago the Baptists of Texas sent a missionary to the cowboys of West Texas. I never heard him called anything but "Brother Milligan." He rode horseback from one ranch to another, with saddlebags bulging with New Testaments and religious tracts. At the "roundups" he held campfire services. He witnessed for his Lord to individuals and preached wherever he could get a group together. He was welcome wherever he went and was held in deep respect and affection by the ranchers and the crews. With the help of the cattlemen and George W. Truett, one of his dreams became a reality. He established a cowboy encampment and named it *Paisano*. The word translated into English has two meanings: "fellow countrymen" or "roadrunner." When I met him he was an old man and reminded me of the pictures I've seen of Moses. His hair and his long beard were snow-white and his shoulders a bit stooped.

One night, after Dr. Truett preached one of his marvelous sermons, Brother Milligan and I walked across the campground toward our one-room houses, which were close together. The stars were unusually bright and I remarked,

"Out here in this high elevation, the stars seem much closer and more brilliant than anywhere I've ever been."

Brother Milligan looked up and then held out his hand to stop me. Still looking at the stars, with a smile he said: "Every time I look at them I think of what a cowboy said to me once. It has been a continual blessing to me. I was with a bunch of cowboys—about thirty of them—at a roundup. One morning when the man who had been riding the night watch over the herd came in, I said to him, 'I heard you singing last night and I marveled how beautiful it sounded and how many songs you know by heart. You repeated only one, "His Eye Is on the Sparrow." Tell me why you sing when you ride around the herd at night. You don't do that in the daytime.'

"He said, 'All of us sing on the night watch. I don't know why it does, but our singing seems to soothe the herd. Brother Milligan, maybe it's because the cattle know that I'm out there and I'm not afraid, so they cease to be afraid, too. They lose their restlessness, stop milling around, and lie down and go to sleep. There is another reason that I sing. Sometime ago you read to us out of the Good Book that the "stars sing" (Job 38:7). They *do* sing. I look up at the heavens and I think of the stars as cowboys—"God's cowboys." I do not mean to be irreverent, but I believe that the "Great Cowboy" puts them out there at night so that in the darkness we may know that he has not forgotten us. They ride the night watch on the human herd, too. Somehow, I feel so secure, I feel so relaxed when I see "God's cowboys" riding the night watch over us humans. He didn't leave us in the dark—he didn't let the sun set and leave us in darkness. He put them up there to tell us that "his eye is on the sparrow" and he cares for you and me.'"

David must have been thinking similar thoughts when he wrote those memorable words, "I will lift up mine eyes unto the hills, from whence cometh my help. My help cometh from the Lord, which made heaven and earth. He will not suffer thy foot to be moved" (Psalm 121:1–3). David testifies that God is gracious and good and has helped him. Quickly he changes *mine* to *thine* and preaches to us. "He will not suffer *thy* foot to be moved: he that keepeth *thee* will not slumber." This thought is found in a number of other psalms also. "He that dwelleth in the secret place of the most High shall abide under the shadow of the Almighty. I will say of the Lord, He is my refuge and my fortress: my God; in him will I trust. For he shall give his angels charge over thee, to keep thee in all thy ways. They shall bear thee up in their hands, lest thou dash thy foot against a stone" (91:1–2; 11–12). There are many messages in this psalm that we need in times like these.

I

Look up.—Remember a famous artist's portrayal of a man sitting all hunched over, his head down, and his hands on each side of his face? It is titled *Despair.*

Jerome K. Jerome, one of our greatest thinkers and writers, expressed it beautifully when he said, "Look up, don't look down. When you look down you see so much of *yourself* and so little of the *other* things that God made. For instance, one day I had a finger that ached in the joint and I decided promptly that I had arthritis. So, I went over to the public library and got a medical book and looked up arthritis. By the time I got through reading two pages, I had arthritis in every joint in my hands, and my knees besides. It scared me and I turned the pages and there was *leukemia*, and I read everything about it. Before I had finished, I knew I had leukemia. I turned the page to *ulcers* and I said, 'So, now I know what causes those pains in my stomach I've wondered about. I've got ulcers.'

"I turned to pellagra, and I just knew I had pellagra. The

only thing I found in that medical book that I didn't have was housemaid's knee, and I wondered why I didn't have that. I went straight to the doctor who had examined me lots of times and had always told me there wasn't anything wrong. When I got there I said, 'I'm a hospital myself, Doctor.' I told him about all of these things I knew I had.

"The doctor sat there for a long time before he said, 'Yes, you're in a bad way. You really are in a bad way, and now that you've diagnosed your case so well, I'm going to give you a prescription. I haven't given you any medicine before, but I'm going to give you a prescription this time and you can take it to the drugstore and get it filled.'

"He wrote it out and folded it up, and I headed for the drugstore. The druggist took the prescription and looked at it. He frowned and made out like he was scratching his head, then he folded it back up and said, 'You know, I'm sorry, but I don't have any of this in my drugstore.'

"I said, 'What? Don't you have the biggest drugstore in this part of the city?'

" 'Yes,' he said, 'but the things the doctor has prescribed for you don't come in a bottle.' He handed it back to me and said, 'You take it and read it for yourself.'

"I opened it and this is what it said, 'Walk eight miles every day, come home and eat a beef steak for supper, and stop reading things you've got no business reading.' It is a dangerous thing to look down at yourself. You get to feeling sorry for yourself."

"I will lift up mine eyes unto the hills." Now, the translators and interpreters had some trouble with this passage of Scripture, because in the Hebrew language there are no commas, no question marks, no exclamation marks, no quotation marks. They weren't sure whether to translate it, "I will lift up mine eyes unto the hills"—with a question after "whence cometh my help," because the next sentence says, "My help cometh from the Lord, which made heaven and earth," or whether to translate it, "I will lift up mine eyes unto the hills whence cometh my help." I think the last reading is right.

"From whence cometh my strength"—David knew from past experience he wasn't going to be able to get along without God and he wasn't going to get along without the help that God would give. I am sure God never intended for any of us to be able to live life at its finest, at its fullest, at its best, without him. He left a place for himself in each of us.

Jesus talks about an empty room. A man decided he did not want the ugly things in his life. He put the devil out and cleaned the room, *and he left it empty*. While David wasn't talking about this thought in Psalm 121, it does remind us that God has left an empty place in our lives for himself. If we dare fill it with material things or leave it empty, we will reap a harvest of havoc. We're going to need him for a partner, we're going to need him for the rough places on life's road. Several times in this psalm David pleads with God to teach him how to live.

C. Oscar Johnson, for many years beloved pastor of Third Baptist Church of St. Louis, Missouri, illustrated this truth with an incident from his boyhood:

"My father was a blacksmith, and I spent much of my time pumping the bellows that made the fire hot. He never bought ready-to-wear horseshoes. He made them. He would put a strip of iron in the fire and leave it until it was white-hot. Then holding it with a pair of tongs, he would bend it around the anvil by tapping it lightly with a hammer. When it was the right shape and size for the horse he was shoeing, he would heat it again and turn the ends down to make the cleats. It seemed so easy that one day when we were not busy I asked him to let me make one. A smile of amusement broke over his face as he answered, 'All right, I'll pump the bellows and you make the shoe.'

"When the strip of iron was hot, I took it off the forge and tried to bend it around the circular end of the anvil. The more I hammered, the funnier it looked. It was twisted and lopsided. I was deeply chagrined. My father took the tongs and held the shoe up. He shook his head and said, 'Son, I never saw the horse that could wear that shoe.' He tossed it back into the fire and after a moment he added, 'Let's make one together.'"

Just so, we need the Heavenly Father to help us when our tasks become too difficult.

II

Whence cometh my help.—Suddenly the state of affairs in our world has become so fearful that security is one of the biggest problems in both our nation and our private lives. I have noticed how quiet and attentive people are when I preach from one of the Bible promises of security. Remember how many times the Labor Unions have threatened to "strike" because the "pension plan" was not satisfactory. They wanted security for old age.

I think one of our noted writers expressed it beautifully when he said, "I was thirty-five years old when I made my first million dollars. I had visions of being one of the wealthy men of the world. I had everything set, and then came the depression and I lost the most of it; it looked like everything was gone. I walked the streets; I was so nervous I didn't want anything to eat. I lost weight, and I was hard to live with. Like Job, I broke out with boils all over my body. They took me to the hospital. The doctors talked with me, tried to reason with me, tried to show me that all was not lost. They pointed out that I still had one of the loveliest Christian wives in the world, and I still had plenty to start on again. I wouldn't listen to them. I couldn't do like Paul, 'forgetting those things which are behind' (Phil. 3:13). I just worried about them.

"Finally, one day the doctor came into my room with a solemn face and said, 'I've got to talk to you pretty seriously. I've got a bit of a shock for you.'

"I said, 'All right, Doctor, what is it?'

"He asked, 'Do you have any relatives that you'd like to send for, that you would like to see? Have you made your will? You have not more than two weeks to live, and I would suggest to you that you use your mind and strength while you have it. Make whatever arrangements you need to make.'

"When my wife came in that morning and I told her what the doctor had said, she sat there silently for a little while and then asked, 'Well, what do you want to do?'

"We made a list of the things that needed to be done. It took us all day and it was late afternoon when we finished. She asked if there was anything she could do before she went home. I said, 'Get me something to eat, then I want to go to sleep. Bring your Bible when you come tomorrow. I want you to read Revelation to me. I'm a Christian. I'm going to spend eternity with God and I want to know what the Bible says about heaven. Revelation has more about heaven in it than any other book, so bring your Bible with you.' She kissed me goodnight. I slept like a log and woke up the next morning hungry for breakfast. She came in and started reading Revelation to me. I went to sleep while she was reading. Four or five days passed in much the same way. I slept and ate; grew quiet and calm.

"Then one morning the doctor came back. He winked at me and said, 'It worked.'

"I said, 'What worked?'

"He said, 'My prescription for you. You wouldn't relax, you wouldn't eat, so I decided to tell you that you weren't going to have anything to worry about, and that you weren't going to be here to suffer from it. You had enough to take care of your wife. Since you knew you were going to die, there wasn't any use to worry about the future, the past, or anything—so you just went to sleep. Now, I can tell you that you are all right. You're going to be fine, and a better man than you were before.'

"Of course, I was stunned at first. I lay there a long time before I said, 'Thank you, Doctor. From now on God's my partner and I won't ever get that way again.' "

How beautifully David is saying it. "I will lift up mine eyes unto the hills, from whence cometh my help." He will not sleep. God will not slumber. Jesus added, "Come unto me, all ye that labour and are heavy laden, and I will give you rest" (Matt. 11:28).

III

A plea for mercy.—The other great message in Psalm 121 is David's plea for mercy. He must have had in mind the great sin he had committed and the day that old Nathan came and pointed his finger in David's face and said, "Thou art the man" (2 Sam. 12:7). The memories of that sin and God's reprimand were never wiped out of David's mind. He was always conscious of the need of God's mercy. Not only this psalm but many others contain this same hunger. He said, "Cleanse thou me from secret faults" (19:12). I think he meant by "secret sins" those faults of which he was not conscious; whatever he meant, he knew that he needed God's continued forgiveness. He knew he needed God to bundle up all of his shortcomings as well as his sins of commission and bury them.

This reminds me of an incident in the life of Guy King. He said there was one unforgettable hour in his first year at college in England. It was New Year's Eve. At eleven o'clock at night all of the students went out on the parade ground and built a huge bonfire. They carried empty boxes from their rooms and gathered wood from everywhere to make one of the biggest bonfires ever.

"We were hilarious," King related. "We sang songs and danced around the fire. Despite the fact that this was an annual affair, I was not prepared for the climax. At five minutes to twelve the headmaster came out. A hush fell over everything. He carried in his hand a small black book. When he held it up and asked, 'Do you know what this is?' there was a groan from all of us. A smile came over his face as he said, 'This book records all of the demerits that have accumulated in the year ending tonight.' He leafed through the pages while we held our breath. He didn't read a single thing aloud. Then he closed the book, stretched his arm out behind him, and with a forward motion tossed it into the middle of the bonfire. The whoop that went up from that crowd of students could have been heard half a mile away. Then the headmaster held up his hand for silence. We listened happily as he said, 'All the records of misdemeanors you committed are destroyed. There is not a black mark anywhere against you. I beg you to keep it that way.' "

It was something like this that was in David's mind. He wanted God to be merciful and also forget all of the things in his past life. Also he knew that only with the strength that God could give would he ever be able to live like God wanted him to live.

12

Open Doors

There came to my office one Monday morning, by appointment, a stranger—a young lady in her thirties. She was well dressed, even expensively so, and cultured.

She said, "I listened to your sermon yesterday morning over the radio and you upset me very much by a statement you made. You quoted from Revelation, 'Behold, I have set before thee an open door, and no man can shut it' (3:8). Then you enlarged on it and stated that God sets before us beautiful doors, like the door of *prayer, fellowship,* and *eternity.* That particular verse has been sort of an anchor to me through the years. I thought it meant that if life got too rough and the burdens became too heavy, you could use this door that God set before you to get out of life. . . . I hope you won't tell me that I was wrong, because this has been a constant source of consolation to me."

To say I was astonished is a huge understatement. I was stunned. As tactfully and carefully as I could, I told her she was wrong. I opened the Bible and read to her what God said to the church at Philadelphia. I tried to explain that God would be greatly displeased if we sought to destroy our bodies.

After she left, I spent a long time thinking about the open doors that God sets before us that *no man can shut*. Before we look at a few of them, we ought to look at that part of the sentence that I have put in italics. There are many doors that men can shut. Let me mention just one.

I think of a boy whom I visited in jail not long ago. He had been sentenced to the penitentiary for six years. He was the only child of a lovely Christian couple, who had sat in my study and wept. Their happiness had been destroyed. Their home was in darkness, because a boy had shut out all of the light and closed some doors in front of them. The law had closed some doors behind him.

I

God sets before us an open door of fellowship with him.—The enemies of Christianity put John, the disciple whom Jesus loved, on a little island called Patmos. One day he wrote, "I looked, and, behold, a door was opened in heaven" (Rev. 4:1). He was isolated from his friends—men could shut those doors and rob him of fellowship with loved ones—but no man could shut the door between him and God.

The enemies of Christianity put Paul and Silas in a dungeon. They shut the iron doors behind them. They cut the lines of communication between them and their friends, but there was a door standing wide open between them and their God. It was a consciousness of this that made it easy for them to pray and sing at midnight. Maybe the reason God sent the earthquake that shook the locked doors open was to assure them that there would always be a door open between them and their God.

No matter what the situation and the circumstances are, no man can keep you from talking to your Heavenly Father. There is always an open door and Jesus' standing invitation says, "Come unto me, all ye that labour and are heavy laden, and I will give you rest. . . . Learn of me . . . and ye shall find rest unto your souls" (Matt. 11:28–29). Again, "Ask, and it shall be given you; seek, and ye shall find; knock, and it shall be opened unto you" (Matt. 7:7). There is an open door between us and God all of the time. And you can pray *when* you will and wherever you are. The doors that men closed on these servants of our Master often were blessings in disguise.

Ollie Edmunds in the little pamphlet "Whatsoever Things" gives us a beautiful example:

"Why was I not exiled before!" exulted Victor Hugo, a score of years after Napoleon III banished him from France. He had been France's most popular literary figure, enjoying tremendous public adulation. Then the sky crashed down on him. Taking exception to some of Hugo's political beliefs, the Emperor sent him into what everybody thought would be oblivion. But during the period of "adversity" Hugo really found himself. In his exile he wrote his most successful novels, including *Les Misérables*, which was published simultaneously in ten languages. He returned to France more famous than when he left.

If somewhere along the line *your* plans are thwarted, if the bottom falls out from under all the things you have been working for, if you come to the place where you have no choice but to start all over again, keep this fellow Hugo in mind. It just *could* be that *you* too may one day exult, "Why didn't this happen to me sooner!"

History is filled with such examples. The important thing is to adopt a receptive attitude—expect some good to come of it all. Even though you can't imagine what on earth it could be, look for it—*confidently*. Be prepared to welcome it—*confidently*, for when the mental climate is right miracles blossom!

II

God sets before us a door to beautiful living.—No matter what the circumstances, your life can still be beautiful. Maybe our greatest witness for Christ is the way we live when the load is heaviest and the pressure is greatest.

Look for a minute at some things in the life of Christ. Many of his sayings that we often quote were spoken in the hour of greatest temptation. One day an enemy said to him, in words that were dripping with honey, "You are a wise teacher. Tell us, is it right to pay tribute to Caesar?" (cf. Matt. 22:16–17). If Jesus had answered yes, the crowd that had been listening to him would have walked away. If he had said no, Pilate's soldiers would have arrested him as a rebel. I have always thought Jesus was smiling when he asked his tempter, "Do you have a coin?" Then holding it in his hand he said, "Whose picture is on this coin?" When he answered, "Caesar's," Jesus handed the coin back to him and spoke those immortal words, "Render therefore unto Caesar the things that are Caesar's; and unto God the things that are God's" (Matt. 22:21).

Another time, "A certain lawyer . . . tempted him, saying, Master, what shall I do to inherit eternal life?" (Luke 10:25). The conversation that followed recorded one of the most beautiful stories that Jesus ever told, the story of the good Samaritan. So, with our lives it is the hour of temptation or trial that gives us the opportunity to witness best for Christ. Let me illustrate.

Disaster came into the home of a young lady. Her father died and her mother was ill. She found that she would have to support the family for awhile. She took an accelerated business course to learn shorthand and typing. When she went to work on her first job, she walked into a big room filled with desks, typewriters, and young lady secretaries. The young ladies were all neatly dressed—in sharp contrast to her plain, old clothes. There had not been enough money for her to buy nice clothes and take the business course, too. Naturally, she was embarrassed. She slipped down low in her chair, hoping the desk would hide her. When lunch time came, she stayed at her desk. She didn't want to be seen. At the close of the day she did not leave until all of the others had gone.

The next morning, as she was getting settled, a young lady named Ann came and sat down on her desk. She, too, was dressed very plainly. Smilingly she said: "Aren't you new here? I didn't see you until yesterday." When she answered in the affirmative, Ann said: "Let's eat lunch together, today."

The young lady relating the experience said: "I eagerly accepted that invitation and we ate lunch together the rest of the week. On Friday, Ann came over smiling, 'This is my payday. Is it yours?' When I told her that it was, she said animatedly, 'Let's go buy some new clothes.'

"All went well for a few weeks and then one morning I found Ann waiting for me with a question: 'Do you still have some of those old dresses?' When I nodded, she pleaded, 'Please wear one of them tomorrow and I'll wear one of mine.' I didn't have to ask her why. Surprise was written all over my face. She said: 'Don't look now, but across the room there is a new girl who is very embarrassed because her clothes are not like ours.'

"The next day, dressed in our old dresses, we went over to the new girl's desk and introduced ourselves and invited her to eat lunch with us. Gratitude, appreciation, love, and relief were in her face as she eagerly accepted. The rest of the week we three ate lunch together.

"Then one day I asked Ann to let me walk home with her. I wanted to talk to her. Her apartment was beautiful and she had a huge wardrobe of expensive dresses. I am sure she read my mind, for she was smiling when I turned to ask, 'You're a Christian, aren't you?' She simply nodded her head."

God sets in front of us open doors for beautiful living, no matter what the circumstances are. When our souls grow beautiful and our hearts are filled with the Spirit of Jesus and our lives have been cleansed by his blood, we will find a way to witness for him.

III

God sets before us an open door to peace of mind.—How can any man ever have peace of mind without the assurance that all is right between him and God? There is born in us a belief in life hereafter. It persists, despite all the learned discourses of the atheists. The most primitive people on earth believe the soul, or the spirit, leaves the body at death and goes on to abide in another place. In the ancient tombs of Egypt archaeologists have found corn and wheat, as well as gold and silver and raiment, placed there for the use of the spirit of the man in the life that followed death. The Indians of our own land buried with a warrior many articles and weapons. In some lands a man's wives were put to death and buried with him. That there is a hereafter is deeply rooted in all of us.

How, then, can a man have peace of mind and face death with assurance and calmness unless he knows that all is well between him and his Maker?

The editor of a newspaper sent Bruce Barton to the hospital to talk to Russell Conwell. Mr. Conwell was coming close to the end of life. Barton found him propped up among the pillows and hesitated to ask him what the editor wanted to know. For a while, he beat around the bush. Finally, Conwell said, "Bruce, come to the point. What do you want?"

With a smile, Bruce hitched his chair up a little closer and said, "Russ, my editor told me that we had printed page after page of your achievements. All the world knows about the seventeen hundred boys that you sent through school and the thousands of times that you delivered your famous lecture "Acres of Diamonds." He wanted me to ask you if there is any fear in your mind as you come close to the end of life."

Dr. Conwell turned his face away for a few minutes and, then looking back at Bruce, smilingly said, "Bruce, when I was a boy of fourteen and lived on a farm in New England, my father said to me one night, 'I have to go to town at daylight in the morning and there are three things that need so much to be done tomorrow. I wish I could help you, for I don't think you can possibly do them all. The bottom land is ready to be plowed, the moisture is just right. Some of the cattle are out of the pasture because they have broken through the fence. The wagon has to be greased because we'll need it to haul corn day after tomorrow. Do the best you can.'

"The next evening, I dragged into the house after dark, just as my father arrived from town. Eagerly he asked: 'How did you make out, Russ?'

"With a bit of pride, I answered, 'I got them all.'

" 'You mean you plowed that field, got the cows back in and fixed the fence, and greased the wagon in one day?' I nodded assent and my father, who was not very demonstrative, came over and put his arm around my shoulders and squeezed me a little. He said: 'A good day's work, Russ.'

"Bruce, I think when I stand before my Heavenly Father he will put his arm around my shoulders and say, 'A good day's work, Russ, a good day's work.' "

Bruce Barton said: "I tipped out of the room. I felt like I had been on holy ground."

We, too, can have this peace of mind and sweet assurance that when we stand before the great Judge, he will say, "A good day's work, son, a good day's work."

13
𝕾nowmen

Thorvaldsen, the great sculptor of the century in which he lived, carved from white marble the most beautiful statue ever made of Jesus. There are replicas of it all over the world. Some of the replicas sell for an astounding amount of money. The original is in Copenhagen and cannot be bought. It has been said that Thorvaldsen's *Christ* has channeled more than five million tourists through Copenhagen. One winter the Prince of Denmark invited him to be his guest at the winter palace for the season. Thorvaldsen accepted under the condition that he might bring with him the piece of marble on which he was presently working. He felt he could not afford to waste that much time, for there were so many pieces of sculpture in his creative mind. The prince answered, "Not only may you bring it, but I'll send for it."

So, his prince set up a studio for him in the winter palace. Thorvaldsen worked every day, even into the night. One morning, at a late breakfast, he and the prince looked out through the big picture windows at the children making a snowman. They had borrowed the prince's long cutaway coat, his high silk hat, his cane, his pipe and his glasses. All went well until they tried to make a face to resemble their handsome prince. Finally, they gave up.

Seeing their downcast faces, the prince said, "You're the master sculptor of the world. Don't you want to go out and help them just a little?"

Thorvaldsen was a perfectionist. He put on his boots and his heavy coat and went out to help make the snowman's face. He asked the prince to stand at the window where he could see him. After packing the snow into a hard ball, he took a sharp chisel and carved out a perfect likeness. It took him three hours. He caught cold and went to bed. That night everything froze. The next morning the sun came out bright and soon the delicately chiseled face and features of the prince were all blurred. The next day when the weather turned warm, the snowman melted and drooped and the likeness was entirely destroyed. It was, as Shakespeare said, "Love's labors lost." Thorvaldsen stayed in bed nearly five weeks with pneumonia, for there was no penicillin in those days.

Years later, when Thorvaldsen died, there appeared this statement by a journalist in Great Britain, "The catastrophe of the century, the disaster of this age, is that Thorvaldsen died before he finished what the connoisseurs declare would have been his masterpiece."

When I read this statement and remembered the snowman, the words of Isaiah came back to me, "Wherefore do ye spend money for that which is not bread? and your labour for that which satisfieth not? Seek ye the Lord while he may be found, call ye upon him while he is near" (55:2, 6). Turn the pages to the New Testament and hear Felix talking to Paul. Felix was trembling when he said, "Go thy way for this time; when I have a convenient season, I will call for thee" (Acts 24:25). Or, listen to Jesus: "Seek ye first the kingdom of God, and his righteousness; and all these things shall be added unto you" (Matt. 6:33). "When he had called the people unto him with his disciples also, he said unto them, Whosoever will come after me, let him deny himself, and take up his cross, and follow me. For whosoever will save his life shall lose it; but whosoever shall lose his life for my sake and the gospel's, the same shall save it. For what shall it profit a man, if he shall gain the whole world, and lose his own soul?" (Mark 8:34–36).

There are three danger messages here.

I

Mistaken magnitudes.—The task of choosing between something good and something better or more valuable is ever before us. There will always be someone tempting us to build a snowman and sometimes we will forget that tomorrow's sun may leave it a blurred blob. We follow the lines of least resistance too easily. We hitch our wagon to a star, but we stop the wagon and climb down when the road gets rough, or we turn aside to enjoy some tempting interlude. We have a dream or we see a vision, but before we make either into a reality too often we stop to build a snowman and time runs out.

One day a man followed Jesus a little way. He was deeply interested and saw a picture of the "good life" spread out before him. So, he said to the Master of life, "I will follow thee, but let me first go and bury my father."

Jesus' answer came back quickly and clear-cut: "Let the dead bury the dead. Come follow me now" (Luke 9:59–60).

Isn't Jesus saying, "Choose now the most important thing. Don't make the mistake of tarrying too long and letting your vision get dim"? Or, maybe you see some good thing you want to do, something you think is of such magnitude you are justified in turning aside, although you have your wagon hitched to that star of your dreams. Then later—too late—you see your mistake. Let me make this live with a true incident.

Margaret Sangster had charge of a good will center among the underprivileged in a big city. One day, speaking to a large audience, she told this experience.

"There came into my big playroom one day a crowd of boys. Among them was one walking on a homemade crutch and a homemade cane. He limped in. One foot turned completely around and faced backwards. His whole body was so twisted he couldn't play with the others, so he backed up against the wall and followed them so hungrily with his eyes that my heart just broke for him. I called him into the office and asked him what had happened. He answered, 'A truck ran over me.' I cleaned him up and made an appointment with a doctor friend who had helped me many times before. The doctor examined him carefully, then called in several other doctors. Finally they said, 'Miss Margaret, we can straighten his leg and arm and a few other things. There is no reason why he can't walk again! It will take several operations. He'd have to stay in the hospital for a long time. The only problem for you now is to get somebody to pay the hospital expenses. We'll do our work gratis—we'll gladly do it for you if you can find somebody to pay the expenses.'

"I picked up the telephone and called the president of one of the banks and told him I needed to see him right away. He said: 'Well, come on down. I've got the president of one of the other banks here with me. Come on, it's just about a block and we will both be glad to see you.' The little boy, on one crutch and a cane, limped with me into the president's office. I told them the story. They looked at each other for a moment, nodded, and then said to me with a smile, 'Go ahead, Miss Margaret, put him in the hospital. We'll see that the bills are paid.'

"The day came when that boy literally danced into my

playroom, and putting his hands on his hips, he pirouetted around. He hopped on one foot and then on the other, then asked, "How'm I doing, Miss Margaret?"

I answered, 'You're doing fine, just fine.' When he had gone, I walked around the playroom with my shoulders up and my head held high with pride. I said to myself, 'Margaret, that's *one thing that you did that you can see*. You are always complaining that you can't see any visible results, and you don't know whether you are accomplishing anything or not. There's *one thing definite* that you can put your finger on that you did.' "

Then Margaret Sangster leaned over the podium and asked: "Where do you think he is today—that boy the doctors and bankers and I straightened out?"

Someone in the audience replied, "He's a preacher." She said: "No."

"A banker?"

"No."

"Governor of the state?"

"No."

"A Senator?"

"No."

"A lawyer?"

Miss Sangster held up her hand for silence and with sadness in her voice said: "You'd never guess. He's in the penitentiary for life for a crime that was so heinous, so terrible, that except for his youth they would have sent him to the electric chair or the gas chamber." After a moment she continued. "Do you see what my mistake was? I spent so much time teaching that boy *how* to walk that I forgot to teach him *where* to walk."

You can fill your time with things that are good, things that are wonderful, things that are splendid, at the expense of things that are finer. "Why spend your money for that which is not bread? your labour for that which satisfieth not." Why don't you seek the Lord while he may be found? Isaiah is saying that there is nothing in this world as important as spending your time doing your God-given assignment.

II

Danger of the convenient.—Some time ago a University of Miami student who was writing a term paper on religion asked me for an interview. "Doctor, what is the biggest enemy to Christianity?" he probed. "What religion is the most competitive as far as Christianity is concerned? Would you say its greatest enemy is communism, Buddhism, Mohammedanism, nazism, secularism, or nationalism? What is it?"

I sat there a moment before answering: "You have named a group of 'isms.' I'd have to coin a word to answer you with an 'ism,' but I would say it is 'convenientism.' So often people put off the decision to accept Christ as Saviour to some more convenient time. They do not intend to stand before God without having made their peace with him, but with Felix they say, 'Some more convenient season, I will send for thee.'"

I remember two incidents I heard George Truett relate when he was preaching to the cowboys and the cattlemen at the Paisano Encampment in West Texas. He was illustrating this very text. The first one was about like this:

"There came rushing into my home one morning, while I was eating breakfast, one of my deacons. His face was terrible to look at. He had a newspaper in his hand. He asked: 'Have you seen the paper?'

"I said: 'No, I haven't.'

"He put a trembling finger on the account of the death of a very prominent banker, and said: 'You know, I'm a banker. This man was in church last Sunday [this was Wednesday], and he listened intently to your sermon. I said to myself,

"Now, the preacher is always telling us to go find somebody
our size, somebody we can talk to, that somebody else can't
talk to. I like this banker and he and I have had lots of business
dealings together. He is a fine man. I'm going to talk to him
tomorrow about giving his life to Christ, and joining our
church." The next morning I got busy—I got awfully
busy—there were so many things that just popped up and I
didn't go to see him. I thought I couldn't leave my bank. So, I
said, "All right, Lord, I'll go in the morning." I didn't even
get lunch Tuesday. Once more there came a deluge of important matters and I didn't get a chance to go. Last night, down
on my knees, I promised the Lord I would go tomorrow—"if
I have to close the First National Bank, I'll see him tomorrow." I picked up the paper this morning and read that he was
dead even when I prayed that prayer last night.'

"This good deacon sat down at the table, put his head down
on his arms and sobbed. Tearfully, he asked, 'Dr. Truett, what
do you think God thinks of me anyhow? I could have led him
to Christ, and I let my life get filled with other things that are
so insignificant and so little by the side of that.' "

The second incident was even more heartbreaking. Let Dr.
Truett tell it:

"A girl of about seventeen died and her father asked me to
conduct her funeral. She was a member of our church, but he
was not. Of course, I agreed to help him with the funeral.
Then he asked: 'Will you ride in my buggy to the funeral? I
want to talk with you.' I consented, and as we rode along to
the cemetery the father said: 'Dr. Truett, when you first came
to town I used to hear you preach every Sunday. I never
missed the Sunday morning service, and I'd literally have to
hold onto the seat in front of me to keep from going up to the
front when you gave the invitation. And when the congregation sang one of those grand old hymns like "Just as I am,

without one plea, but that thy blood was shed for me," I just had to hold onto the bench in front of me. After the service, I would walk the streets for hours. I was miserable. Along about two or three o'clock in the afternoon, I'd sort of pay myself off with a promissory note. I would promise myself and promise God that next Sunday—next Sunday—I would take my place on the side of Jesus Christ. I'd give my life to him. I'd join the church. Next Sunday would come and I'd go to church, but when the invitation hymn was sung, I froze. I couldn't step out into the aisle, I just couldn't do it. Dr. Truett, I know you are a better preacher now than you were then, but when I hear you preach now it doesn't move me at all. What's happened? Has something happened to me?'

"I didn't have the heart to tell him that there is a line, unseen by men, that when you've crossed it you've built such a thick barrier around your life, your mind, your heart, and your will that you'll never let Jesus in. You have not sought the Lord while he was near, while he could be found. . . . You have passed the point of no return."

III

Danger of the immediate.—It is so easy to forget the ultimate in the press of the immediate. We get absorbed in the present and don't take the "long look." Often *one tree* can keep you from seeing the forest if you stand close enough to it.

There is a verse in Ecclesiastes which reads, "Better is the end of a thing than the beginning" (7:8). The word "better" in the Hebrew means of more value or is more important and more precious. How much better it would have been if Thorvaldsen had paused a moment and realized the risk he was running. The world of art has paid a huge price for that snowman. Too many of us have spent our labor for that which does not satisfy and our money for that which is not bread.

Esau, hungry, fatigued, and famished, comes to his brother's camp. The odor of a savory dish drifts out to meet him. He hurries and begs for a big helping now, right now. His cunning brother says nonchalantly, "Give you all you want for your birthright." Esau falls for the immediate. Apparently he gives no thought for the future. "Give it to me—if I starve now, what's important about the future?" Before we condemn him, we would do well to make this personal. Have not all of us wanted something so urgently that we mortgaged the future to satisfy some hunger of the present?

Abraham and Lot came to the parting of their ways. Abraham, the great soul that he was, said to Lot, "There are the valleys and here are the hills—you take your choice, you go one way and I will go the other." Lot looked at the lush green grass of the valleys and then at the barren hills. Maybe he could see Sodom and Gomorrah in the distance. Maybe he even knew that they were dens of iniquity. He may have known that eventually they would have brimstone and fire rained on them and that the valleys would end. But that was a long way off, and right in front of him there was plenty. Maybe he said to himself, "Let the future take care of itself, I'll eat and drink and make merry for a while." Again, let us not condemn him too quickly—not before we turn back a few pages of our own lives.

These three dangers are *real*. We need the warning, but we should not stop there. God didn't. Read the rest of the passage, "Hearken diligently unto me, and eat ye that which is good, and let your soul delight itself in fatness. . . . Hear, and your soul shall live. Seek ye the Lord while he may be found" (Isa. 55:2–3,6). Isaiah doesn't stop with the *don't*'s. In the same breath he implores us to listen carefully that our souls might live and be "delighted with the delicacies" that the Lord will give us.

14
A Mustard Seed and a Woman's Song

Bishop Thoburn, Methodist missionary to India, was walking down the street of the city in which his mission was located. A large feather of an eagle drifted to the ground in front of him. He searched the sky for the eagle, but there was no sign of him. Turning the feather over and over in his hands, he recalled that our forefathers had made pens out of such feathers and some historic documents had been signed with those pens. Curious to see if this feather would write, he hurried to his study, took a sharp knife and sliced across the heavy end of the feather. It wrote so beautifully he decided on the spur of the moment to write a letter to his sister, Isabella, in Boston. He wrote of something he had been turning over in his mind for a long time. He told of how mistreated and neglected the girls and women of India were and that he felt God would hold us responsible if we did nothing about it.

Then he wrote: "You are a schoolteacher. Although you are excellent, there are thousands of others in America who could take your place. Why don't you come over here and start a school for the girls and women who come to my compound to church?"

Isabella read that letter to the Woman's Missionary Society of her church. Spontaneously the members responded. They told her if she would go, they would finance the whole project. Thus started the first Christian school for girls in India. It has done much to enhance womanhood. Today it is a huge institution and continues to lift the level of life for those who live in that part of the world.

After reading this incident and marveling that so small a thing as a feather drifting out of the blue sky would bring such a blessing, it was just a step to open my Bible to the thirteenth chapter of Matthew. Here I read the words of Jesus: "The kingdom of heaven is like to a grain of mustard seed, which a man took, and sowed in his field: Which indeed is the least of all seeds: but when it is grown, it is the greatest among herbs, and becometh a tree, so that the birds of the air come and lodge in the branches thereof" (vv. 31–32).

Matthew said, "Without a parable spake he not unto them" (v. 34). Evidently Jesus realized there was no other way to describe the kingdom of God and nowhere else did he so graphically do so. Perhaps he also realized there was no other way for him to hold their attention. The events in every story he told were familiar to them. He used no big words. Each parable painted a picture of some part of the kingdom he came to establish on earth. It is significant that three of the stories in this chapter have as their center a seed. The one quoted above puts the emphasis on a *tiny* seed. This suggests three things:

I

God often uses little things to accomplish big results.—The tiny seed grew into the largest herb. The same design can be traced through Christ's actions while he lived on earth. God has not changed his plan. We can see this pattern everywhere today. Many of his miracles present the same pattern. Look at this. A crowd of excited people pressed forward to listen to a man who seemed to be signing his own death warrant. His name was Simon Peter, and he was definitely accusing the people of Jerusalem and the powerful Pharisees of crucifying God's own Son. About three thousand believed him and repented. A few days later this same Simon Peter stood on Solomon's porch and again a crowd pressed close, this time that they might see a lame man who had been healed. Again the fearless disciple accused them of putting to death the Prince of peace. Some five thousand believed and repented. How did this thing happen? Turn the calendar back about three years and read this account.

Jesus went down to the Sea of Galilee. A crowd gathered. He stopped to talk to them. The people in the back could not hear, so they crowded forward until Jesus stood on the very edge of the Sea of Galilee. Jesus turned and saw two boats pulled up against the shore. He stepped into one of them. Did it just happen to be Simon Peter's boat? No, not at all. I think Christ knew it would be this way a long time before he went down to the Sea of Galilee. Purposely he chose Simon's boat, and said to him, "Pull it out just a little way from shore so I can see the faces of the people that are here." Simon sat in the boat and held it still and listened. This is where Pentecost started. Truth, like a little mustard seed, was planted in his heart. It often happens this way today. Let me illustrate.

A true story was recently written for *Reader's Digest*, titled "My Most Unforgettable Character." The author was a murderer but had been led to Christ and even into the gospel ministry by a country preacher. For nearly forty years Josiah Elliott, the country preacher, had prayed one prayer: "Lord, let me have one, please Lord, let me have one city church. Don't keep me a country preacher all my life. Let me have one city church." God kept him in the country! One by one the boys came out of his churches and went away to college, to the seminary, and on to preach the gospel of Christ. One of the boys he had led to Christ led George W. Truett to Christ; another led Casper Warren to Christ. Both of these men have served as president of the Southern Baptist Convention!

Thus, again we see that many times one life that seems so insignificant, one tiny mustard seed, can be so important. Out of little beginnings God builds the kingdom. The words that you say to somebody may be in the Master's plan. The call that you make, the person that you lead to Christ, or that class that you teach may be a part of the Master's design.

Most of us know something of the wonderful missionary achievements of the Scudder family. John Scudder was practicing medicine here in America. A child patient could not live through the night. The big-hearted doctor decided to stay with the family until the end came. Sitting beside the bed, he noticed on the wall of the room a large map of India, into which had been stuck white-headed pins, indicating the location of every medical missionary. There was only one medical missionary for every 350,000 people. In the days that followed, Dr. Scudder could not forget those white-headed pins. They even intruded his sleep. Finally he and his wife went to India. Nine children were born to them. They all became missionaries, and so did their children. To date, the Scudder family has served more than one thousand missionary years. Tiny pins became mustard seeds that grew into the largest herbs.

II

The amazing power of growth.—Socrates once said, "Man is born incomplete in an unfinished world." Thousands of years later someone said, "When I pray, 'Give us this day our daily bread,' God gives me a handful of seed and directs me to a field in which to sow them."

Jesus told Nicodemus, "You must be born again" (John 3:7). Of course, we too must be born again, but we will not be born full-grown Christians. It may take many years before we touch the fringe of the command that Jesus gave his disciples, "Be ye therefore perfect, even as your Father which is in heaven is perfect" (Matt. 5:48). Paul said to some young Christians, "I have fed you with milk, and not with meat: for hitherto ye were not able to bear it, neither yet now are ye able" (1 Cor. 3:2). Let me illustrate:

Mr. Wagner was born on the shore of the Chesapeake Bay and had spent his life tonging oysters. In my first pastorate after seminary one of my deacons took me down to the Fish Market, where this physical giant had a thriving business. He had been led to Christ in one of Billy Sunday's services but had never joined any church. So appreciative was he of our call that he could not find enough nice things to do for us. He joined our church and for the first time began studying the Bible. At the first business meeting he attended, one of the recommendations met with some opposition. One man got emotional and said some unkind things. Mr. Wagner was sitting up front taking it all in. Finally, he walked up to me and in a stage whisper said, "You want that I should throw him out?" A roar of laughter followed and the tension was broken. Mr. Wagner was like Paul said, "a babe in Christ," but he grew, oh, how he grew. He became one of the great leaders in his church and in the Baptist work of the state.

There is another truth about this tiny mustard seed that Jesus very succinctly stated in another place. "Except a corn of wheat fall into the ground and die, it abideth alone: but if it die, it bringeth forth much fruit. He that loveth his life shall lose it; and he that hateth his life in this world shall keep it unto life eternal" (John 12:24–25). So, if this is to be "the largest of all herbs," the mustard seed must obey the "sacred

law of sacrifice." It must lose its life. Jesus is making it plain
that this law of the plant world has its counterpart in the
human world. Jesus is speaking here, not only of himself, but
of all of us. Not one of us would have grown up had not some
others given up at least a part of their lives.

A fellow pastor told a group of us recently of a young lady
who had gone from one of his churches to a seminary to
prepare to be a missionary. While there, her sister died and left
three small children. She left the seminary and gave the next
fifteen years of her life to those children. They all grew up
and volunteered for the mission field. He concluded, "God
needed three missionaries instead of one." The sacred law of
sacrifice can be seen everywhere.

III

Satan copied God's design.—It is a well-known fact that
only valuable things are counterfeited. No counterfeiter today
would waste his time and talent counterfeiting Confederate
money. They try and are sometimes successful in counterfeiting five- and ten-dollar bills. The FBI says there are in
circulation today thousands of dollars in counterfeit money.
Hardly a day passes in Miami that some of the bogus bills are
not intercepted by the banks of the city.

Is it any wonder that Satan would use the valuable pattern
that has been so successful in the establishment of the kingdom
of God? Even before Christ came to earth, this plan of God
was often seen. The Old Testament is full of incidents of this
very thing.

God sent Samuel to Jesse's plantation to anoint one of the
sons of this man of God to be king. Jesse paraded in front of
Samuel, one by one, his stalwart, full-grown sons. When
Samuel looked at the first one presented, Eliab, he said,
"Surely the Lord's anointed is before him" (1 Sam. 16:6). But

God said to Samuel a thing that we should forever remember, "Look not on his countenance, or on the height of his stature; because I have refused him: for the Lord seeth not as man seeth; for man looketh on the outward appearance, but the Lord looketh on the heart" (v. 7).

Then Jesse had the other seven young giants to pass in front of Samuel. When God said, "None of these," the old prophet was a bit dumbfounded—and so was Jesse. Puzzled, Samuel asked, "Are here all thy children?" (v. 11).

Jesse answered, "There remaineth yet the youngest [just a boy] . . . he keepeth the sheep."

God chose "the smallest"—David.

Satan was present that day and saw it all. Patiently he waited for his chance to use the method. It came.

A war broke out between the Israelites and the Philistines. There was a giant among the Philistines who came out every day and shouted to the Israelite army that he would fight any man in the army, and said, "If I whip you, then all of you will be our slaves. If you whip me, then all of the Philistines will be your slaves, and we won't have to have a battle." But there was no one who would accept the challenge.

Now David, the stripling, had gone down to visit his brothers in the army, and when he heard that challenge, you know what happened. He took those five little stones and with his slingshot buried one of them in the giant's forehead. He was victorious and all the Philistines fled.

When the Israelite army marched home, the women came out to meet them, for the runners had brought the story to them. They lined both sides of the road along which the army marched. They sang improvised songs.

Here was Satan's chance. Some woman had to think of these words (what a pity): "Saul has slain his thousands, David his ten thousands." The crowd picked it up and chanted it. Up until then, David was riding with Saul and Saul was so happy and proud to have him. Saul was going to take him forever into his palace. David was to live there. Jonathan had fallen in love with him, and they had become fast friends. Everything was wonderful. Satan put a little rhyme, a little piece of song, in a woman's mind and everybody picked it up.

A little imp, not larger than a mustard seed, a little green imp of jealousy was born in the mind of Saul. The tiny imp grew and it was just a little while until Saul was exerting all of his energy, all of his life, everything in the world that he had to the killing of David, the hero.

J. B. Phillips translates James 3:5, "A whole forest can be set ablaze by a tiny spark of fire." W. M. Elliott once preached a searching sermon from this text. Said he, "the third chapter of James's epistle talks about the damage which an undisciplined tongue can do. While the tongue itself is small in size, it can be terrific in its consequences. It is like a little spark of fire which, though tiny and insignificant in itself, can become a blazing forest. The tiny spark is important, not because of its size, but because of its possibilities."

> So don't despise the little things
> Which happen daily round us,
> For some of them may
>   take wings
> To startle and confound us.

Men do not become evil all at once. The descent is gradual.

Most people have fortified themselves against the great sins, but few have built up any defense against the small defections. There is a passage in Charles Dickens' *Oliver Twist* which illustrates this. Bill Sikes and his companions have come to a house which they plan to burglarize. They have with them little, timid, shivering Oliver Twist. Bill shows Oliver a small latticed window several feet above the ground at the back of the house, a window so small that no one thought of locking it.

"Now, listen, you young limb," said Bill, "I'm going to put you through. Take this light, go up the steps, along the hall to the street door and open it."

Only a latticed window, very small—so small that the residents thought it not worth securing. But it was large enough for frail Oliver to get through, and Oliver was big enough to run down the hall and admit Bill Sikes and his evil companions. So, we are fortified against the Bill Sikeses of sin but not against the Oliver Twists. They get in, and lo, all are admitted.

> Who is it knocks so loud?
> A little lonely sin,
> Slip through, we answer—
> And all hell is in.

The book of Ecclesiastes says: "Let us hear the conclusion of the whole matter" (12:13). Christ is putting the emphasis on the potential of little things. The kingdom of God may be planted in our hearts by a single sentence that someone speaks to us; or, the kingdom may be planted in the life of someone else by a little word we say. In Proverbs we read, "A word fitly spoken is like apples of gold in pictures [baskets] of silver" (25:11). When Jesus explained the parable of the sower to his disciples, he began, "The sower soweth the word" (Mark 4:14).

Likewise, and what a pity, some small act of yours or mine or some careless, thoughtless word may blast a soul into eternal death.